CAESAR
DE BELLO GALLICO V

Edited with Introduction,
Notes and Vocabulary by

R.C. Carrington

Bristol Classical Press

First published in 1939 by G. Bell & Sons Ltd
under the editorship of R.C. Carrington, M.A.,D.Phil.
in the Alpha Classics Series

This edition published in 1984 by
Bristol Classical Press
an imprint of
Gerald Duckworth & Co. Ltd
61 Frith Street
London W1D 3JL
e-mail: inquiries@duckworth-publishers.co.uk
Website: www.ducknet.co.uk

Reprinted 1992, 2001

A catalogue record for this book is available
from the British Library

ISBN 0-86292-136-8

PREFACE

THIS edition of the fifth book of Caesar's *Gallic War* follows, in general treatment, the lines of *Caesar's Invasions of Britain*. Stress is laid primarily on the elucidation of the subject-matter, and points of syntax and grammar are only explained in the Notes if they would not normally be met in a School Certificate course of composition. The editor would like to acknowledge his debt to Rice Holmes, *Caesar's Conquest of Gaul*; Jullian, *Histoire de la Gaule*; Constans, *César, Guerre des Gaules*; Parker, *The Roman Legions*; Collingwood and Myres, *Roman Britain and the English Settlements*; and to the Oxford University Press for permission to use the text of Du Pontet in the *Oxford Classical Texts*.

R. C. C.

May 1939.

CONTENTS

LIST OF ILLUSTRATIONS

PLATES

(Following p. 24)

INTRODUCTION

I. Ancient Gaul

This book deals with two subjects—Caesar's second invasion of Britain, which took place in the summer of 54 B.C. and the revolt which broke out in north Gaul during the following winter. In this and the next two sections, three questions will be dealt with: (i) What was Gaul like in Caesar's time? (ii) What was Britain like? (iii) By what steps did Rome carry her arms to the English Channel and what was in Caesar's mind in bringing them across?

Gaul in the time of Caesar was in the main a Celtic country. The original home of the Celts had been east of the Rhine, but during the sixth century B.C. this home was invaded by Nordic peoples from south Sweden and Denmark. Before this pressure most of the inhabitants migrated. Some moved into north-east France and settled in Champagne, and here they overcame the existing population and developed a culture characterised by graves in which the chieftains were buried with their chariots and armour. A century or so later their descendants were to introduce this culture into north-east Britain (p. 6). Others went to south-west France and mingled with the Iberian inhabitants to form the Aquitanians of later times. The chief place of settlement, however, was in Central Gaul, from the Cévenne Hills and the River Garonne to the River Seine, where they completely subjugated the existing peoples and Celticised the country. Here in course of time the richest and most powerful Celtic kingdoms grew up—those of the Arverni, the Aedui, the Bituriges, the Carnutes, and the Sequani—some of which at various times attempted without success to unify the Celtic peoples under their own domination.

A remnant of the original Celts stayed east of the Rhine and, mingling with the Nordic invaders, formed the Belgic peoples. Towards the end of the second century B.C. these peoples invaded the area of Belgium and brought to an end the culture which their ancestors had established there 400 years before. The Belgic tribes spoke a different dialect from the other Celts and were also markedly more warlike. In the first half of the first century B.C., they crossed to Britain and overran its south-east corner (p. 6).

Thus in Caesar's time Gaul was divided into three large regions—Celtic Gaul proper, Aquitania, and Belgium. Each region had many different tribes within it, and though attempts had been made to bring them into some sort of unity, these attempts had failed through their mutual jealousies. Tribal rivalry played a prominent part in the events which led up to the intervention of Caesar in Gaul, for in 61 B.C. the Sequani invited Ariovistus, a German chieftain, to help them against the Aedui, who were, in consequence, crushingly defeated; and in 58 B.C. the Aedui in their turn sought the help of a Swiss tribe, the Helvetii, and it was against the threat of the latter people that Caesar intervened. One unifying influence in the country was the Celtic religion, which was presided over by the Druids. Each year in the forest of Orleans a solemn meeting was held, and it was attended by representatives of many tribes. Though primarily religious, the meeting must have inspired a consciousness of racial unity. Nevertheless it was true that only conquest by a foreign power could reconcile the rival tribes, and the achievement of Caesar in unifying Gaul was perhaps his greatest contribution to history.

The Gauls had originally been organised in clans (*pagi*), and such organisation still prevailed among the Aquitani. But elsewhere the clans had coalesced into tribes, which Caesar calls *civitates*. Towns existed—fortified strongholds to which the population could retire when attacked—but tribal influence proved strong, and in the long run it was not the name of the town that tended to survive, but the name of the tribe. Thus the Agedincum of Caesar's day became Sens after the Senones, Avaricum became Bourges after the Bituriges, and Samarobriva became Amiens after the Ambiani. The government had been in the hands of kings, but in Caesar's time kings were the exception rather than the rule, having been replaced for the most part by aristocracies under elected magistrates. Attempts were sometimes made to restore the old dynasties, and strife between the noble families was common. Caesar himself more than once profited by such discord to set up a client king and put one party or the other under obligation to himself. The mass of the people—the population hardly numbered more than seven million—lived obscure and laborious lives in villages of the same general type as their counterparts in Britain (p. 5).

The land was more thickly covered with forest than it is to-day. At the present time, forest covers about one-sixth of the total area of the country, but in ancient times it is estimated that it covered more than two-thirds, and it plays an important part in Caesar's narrative. Hunting and fishing were the normal means of livelihood, with cattle-breeding in the hilly regions and corn-growing on the plains. Gallic metal-work was of a high order, and there was a widely developed system of commerce. They had coined money since the first half of the third century B.C., when they had drawn their types from coins of Philip of Macedon, which had been introduced through Marseilles. In the process of being copied a great number of times the types became much debased and almost unrecognisable (Pl. II, *b*).

Though their infantry was numerous, the mainstay of the Gallic army lay in the cavalry. Chariots had previously been used in warfare, but in Caesar's time, though their use still continued in Britain, their place had been taken by cavalry on the continent (p. 89). Only the leaders wore defensive armour, while the common soldiers were clad in tunic and trousers, with a cloak thrown over their shoulders, and were thus a poor match for the heavily armed Roman troops. In temperament, tactics, and military knowledge, too, they were inferior to the Romans. Their first onslaught was furious, but if it was withstood their fury quickly evaporated. They lacked skill in choosing positions, in constructing fortifications, and in siege warfare, although in these respects they quickly learnt their assailant's methods. Thus in the attack on the camp of Q. Cicero, which is described in chs. XXXVIII–LII, their siege-works, learnt from Roman prisoners, were such as to evoke the admiration of Caesar (ch. LII, 2). The chief military weakness of the Gauls was due to their lack of political cohesion, for their tribal divisions made it difficult for them to make a levée en masse, and, unless held together by a strong personality like Vercingetorix, their armies tended to disband after an initial defeat. In the struggle with Caesar the advantage which the Gauls had in numbers was more than counterbalanced by their inability to place the welfare of the nation above their petty rivalries.

II. Ancient Britain

Compared with Gaul, Britain in Caesar's time was something of a backwater. All the tribes seem to have spoken Celtic—at any rate no certain survivals of a pre-Celtic language have been found—but they were not all Celtic by race and they had entered the country from diverse directions and at various times.

At the end of the Bronze Age (roughly about 1000 B.C.), Britain was inhabited by peasants who lived mainly on the gravels of river banks or on the light soils of the chalk downs of the southern counties and of the limestone plateau of the Cotswolds. They lived, not in towns (of which there were none), but in villages, composed of groups of huts surrounded by small fields of the same type as is illustrated in Pl. I. Their ploughs were light and primitive, suitable for the soils on which they lived, but unsuitable for the heavier soils of the river valleys. They made rough clay pottery of their own but knew the use of bronze for arms (*e.g.* swords, spear- and axe-heads), agricultural implements (*e.g.* sickles and the fittings of carts), and domestic utensils (*e.g.* buckets and cauldrons), all of which they bought from itinerant vendors who made them at suitable centres or imported them from the continent.

The first Iron-Age invaders, the forerunners of the Celts, came during the seventh and sixth centuries B.C., probably from Holland and Champagne. Their remains are found mostly in the S.E. of the country, but they cover a long coast-line, from Yorkshire to Dorset, and stretch in a north-westerly direction as far as the Cotswolds. Many of these invaders continued to live in hut-villages, like those of the Bronze-Age inhabitants, but they also introduced a new type of settlement, known to archaeologists as the 'hill-fort.' These were small towns with dwellings inside them, permanently inhabited and protected by a rampart and a ditch. Further invasions followed, not this time in the S.E., which continued to be dominated by the first wave, but in the S.W. and N.E. In the S.W., the tin-mines of Cornwall began about 400 B.C. to attract traders from Spain. But soon the Veneti of Brittany, who in Caesar's time were to claim a monopoly of the cross-Channel trade between Brittany and S.W. England, cut the communications between England and Spain, and thereafter settlers from Brittany invaded Dorset and Somerset. In the N.E. peoples of a similar culture landed in the East Riding of Yorkshire. They came from the district of the Seine and the Marne in France, and one tribe of them bore the significant name Parisii. The most characteristic monuments of the south-western peoples are the massive and intricately constructed hill-forts in which they lived; those of the north-eastern peoples are the graves in which their chiefs were buried complete with chariots and armour. The difference in the nature of these remains is typical of a difference of political conditions. In the S.W. the invaders settled down with the existing inhabitants in a peaceful town-life; in the N.E. they formed a ruling aristocracy. Starting from the coasts by which they entered, these cultures spread inland on the fringe of the earlier Iron-Age culture that still dominated the S.E. and they finally met in the Midlands.

The last of the early Iron-Age invasions occurred in the first half of the first century B.C., shortly before the expeditions of Caesar. The invaders were the Belgae, that mixed people, partly of Celtic, partly of German blood which had occupied Belgic Gaul towards the end of the second century B.C. and came to Britain, first, as Caesar says, to plunder and then to settle (v, 12). They landed in Kent and round the mouth of the Thames, and spread in a north-westerly direction over Hertfordshire and Essex. Their importance in developing the civilisation of Britain was very great, and among the new features which they introduced several are specially significant for an understanding of Caesar's narrative. (i) They brought over the use of a stronger plough than the pre-existing inhabitants had used and were thus able, after clearing the forests which had filled the river valleys down to that time, to till the heavier soils which lay there. (ii) They continued the tradition of building hill-forts but built them, not, like the earlier invaders, on the open downland, but on thickly wooded hills such as Bigbury near Canterbury or Wheathampstead near St. Albans, lying in the heavy forest-land which they were engaged in clearing. (iii) They sprinkled the land as they cleared it with houses of a type which the Romans called 'villae'—isolated dwellings with all the equipment of well-to-do farms standing in the centre of their own land. It is not surprising that in both his expeditions Caesar seems to have found plenty of corn to pillage for the upkeep of his army. (iv) They introduced coinage into Britain. Previously the only form of currency for whose use there is any evidence consisted of iron bars of various weights (Pl. II, *a*), many specimens of which have been found in the south-west counties. The Belgae brought coins with them from Gaul, and later they began to strike coins on the spot (Pl. II, *b*, i).

Such in brief outline was the history of the invasions of Britain before the time of Caesar. They had left the country divided into different cultural bands. In Kent, Hertfordshire, and Essex were the newly

Map of South East Britain
to illustrate Caesar's Invasion

TRINOBANTES
ISLE OF THANET
Richborough
(Rutupiae)
Pegwell Bay
Bigbury
Canterbury
(Durovernum
Cantiacorum)
edway
G. Stour
L. Stour
Sandwich
Deal
Walmer
Kingsdown
South Foreland
Dover
(Dubris)
D
Wissant
Ambleteuse
Boulogne
(? Portus Itius)
Scale of Miles
0
10
20
30
40

arrived Belgic peoples. To the south of them, working the iron of the Sussex Weald, and also to the north of them round the Wash and to the west, forming a fringe along their frontier, lay the descendants of the first wave of Iron-Age invaders that had come from Holland and Champagne. Among them were tribes whose names we know—the Trinobantes, Iceni, and Regni—of whom the former, situated in Essex, are stated by Caesar to have been constantly at war with the great Belgic chief Cassivellaunus (v, 20). Farther west lay a peaceful and prosperous region, inhabited by the descendants of the peoples who from the fourth century onwards had invaded Dorset and Somerset from Brittany. They were now more highly developed artistically than the Belgae, though behind them in agricultural skill. Across the Midlands they joined hands with a people of like culture, warlike offspring of that warrior aristocracy that hailed originally from the valleys of the Seine and the Marne. At this time they were laying the foundation of the military power of the Brigantes, destined to cause the Romans much trouble in later years. On the western and northern edges of the country lay primitive peoples, in a very backward state of civilisation, still carrying on the manner of life that was typical of the whole country at the end of the Bronze Age. The use of iron was still strange to them and they themselves were little known to the civilised world.

III. The Roman Background (Map, page 13)

In 58 B.C., when Caesar took over the command of Gaul, Rome's northern frontier stretched in an ill-defined line from the Pyrenees to the Black Sea. Caesar's command lay in the western half of this frontier, from the Pyrenees along the Alps to

Illyricum and embraced three provinces, Gallia Cisalpina, Gallia Transalpina, and Illyricum. (1) After much ebb and flow, the dominion of Rome had been pushed to the Alps in the first half of the second century B.C., though 'Cisalpine Gaul,' from the Alps to the Rubicon, was not established as a separate military command till a century later. (2) The coast district of Illyria had been annexed by Rome in 167 B.C. after the Macedonian wars, though here too no regular governor was sent for another century. (3) To the west of the Alps, a corridor of territory had been acquired along the south coast of France—'Transalpine Gaul'—as a result of successful wars against the Ligurians and Allobroges which ended in 121 B.C.

The frontier of these provinces was exceedingly weak. In the central portion the Alps, though a fearsome barrier at first glance, really invite invaders by their easy gradients from the north side and their swift descent to the south; and to the east and west there was no recognisable frontier at all. Rome's neighbours were loosely organised tribes of unsettled habits, liable to rise up suddenly in search of fresh lands and periodically to invade Roman territory. A double movement of this kind took place in the late 'sixties' of the first century B.C. and was the occasion of Caesar's intervention in Gaul. First a horde of Germans, led by Ariovistus, invaded the rich plain of eastern France, and then a Celtic tribe, the Helvetii, issuing from its home in Switzerland prepared to cross the Rhône near Geneva and to traverse the Roman corridor on its way to western France (p. 2). It was at this point that Caesar came on the scene with four legions (58 B.C.); he reached Geneva just in time to stop the Helvetii, drove them back to their homes, and then expelled the Germans too.

Down to 61 B.C., when he went as pro-praetor to Spain, Caesar's reputation was that of a talented but rakish democrat, who had had as yet no opportunity of conducting military campaigns on any considerable scale. He was forty-one years of age at the time, late in life to become conscious of a hitherto unsuspected military capacity; yet it seems quite certain that it was his Spanish command which made him realise for the first time his real military ability. Thereafter his chief desire was to obtain the consulship and through it, as pro-consul, a province of the first class. In 59 B.C., with the support of Pompey, Rome's leading general, and Crassus, her leading financier, he became consul and, despite the opposition of the senate, was assigned the Gauls and Illyricum as his province.

In the winter 58–57 B.C., after routing the Helvetii, Caesar stationed his legions outside the Roman province, thus conveying a hint to the Gauls that their day was drawing near. The conquest of Gaul was however to take eight years, and even so, its final organisation into provinces had to be left to his adopted son and successor, Augustus.

The eight years of his campaigning fall into three groups: (1) 57–56 B.C., in which he quickly overran the whole of Gaul, and carried his arms to the Channel and the Rhine; (2) 55–54 B.C., the years of his forays into Germany and Britain; (3) 53–50 B.C., the period in which Gaul was really subjugated, relentlessly and finally.

(1) In 57 B.C., with six legions in all, Caesar broke the back of a coalition of the Belgic tribes, while his *legatus*, Publius Crassus, with a separate detachment, moved down the Atlantic coast and overran it from Normandy to the Garonne. In the next year Caesar crushed the Veneti of Brittany who, though they had submitted in 57, reasserted their inde-

pendence in 56, seeing in Caesar's arrival a threat to their carrying trade across the Channel. He occupied all the northern seaboard between Brittany and Flanders, while Crassus pushed his way through Aquitania to the Pyrenees.

MAP TO ILLUSTRATE CAESAR'S PROVINCES

(2) By the beginning of 55 B.C., 'Gaul was, to all appearance, conquered.' * The appearance was to prove illusory, but on the strength of it Caesar made expeditions into Germany and Britain. The occasion of his invasion of Germany was an incursion into northern Belgium of two German tribes, the Usipetes

* Rice Holmes, *Caesar's Conquest of Gaul*, p. 95.

MORINI
R. Scheldt
ATREBAT
Boulogne
St Pol
AMBIANI
R. Somme
Amiens
BELLOVACI
Montdidier
R. Ai
Champlieu
R. Seine
R. Mar
ESUBII
CARNUTES
SENONE

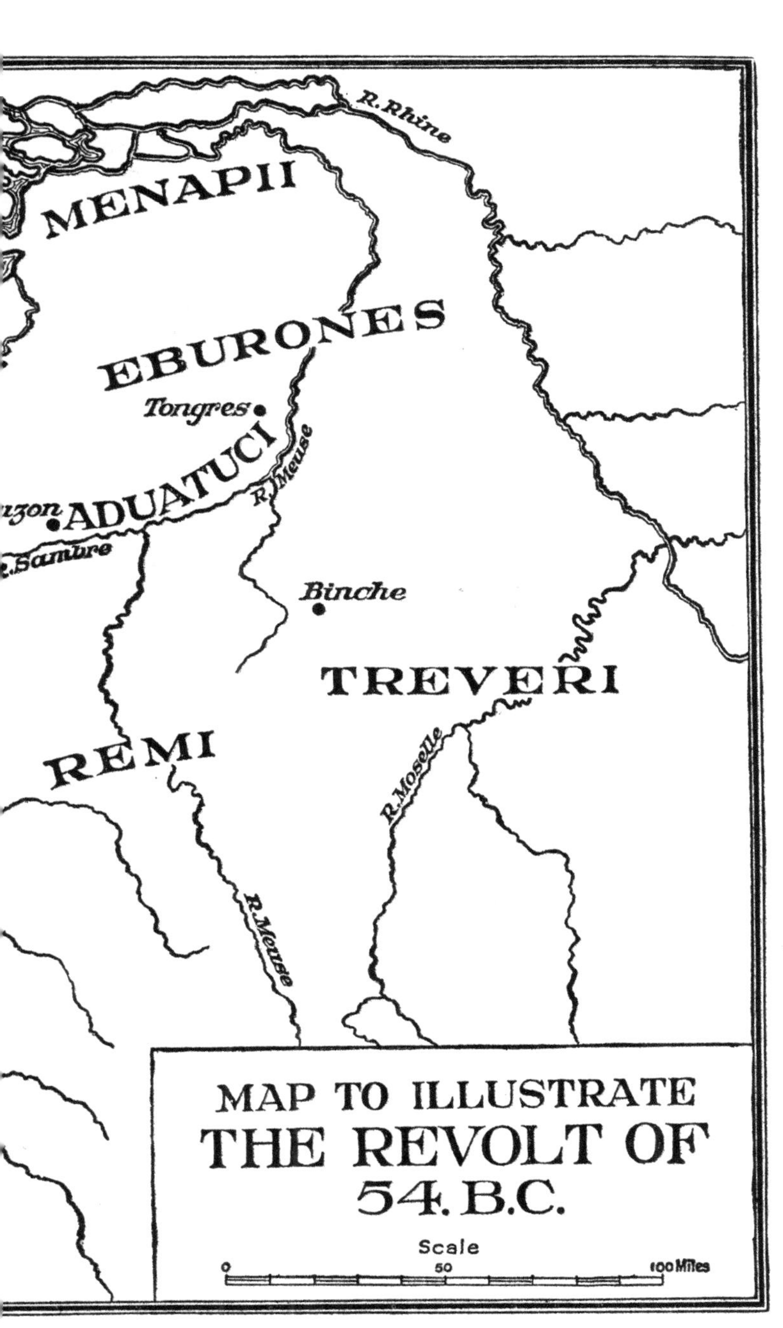

MAP TO ILLUSTRATE
THE REVOLT OF
54. B.C.

and Tencteri. He succeeded in annihilating them and followed up the massacre by crossing the Rhine. We do not know whether he had in mind the conquest of Germany or merely a foray to overawe the German tribes and prevent further incursions. If his idea was conquest, he soon abandoned it, for the German tribes withdrew into the interior without offering battle and Caesar did not pursue them far. He was back in Gaul in less than three weeks. Then, despite the lateness of the season—it was August—he made a preliminary expedition to Britain with two legions. Here again he does not tell us what his ultimate intentions were—whether, that is, he intended to conquer the whole island or part of it, or merely to overawe the tribes who had been sending help to his enemies in Gaul. He does indeed imply that the latter, as well as the need for making a reconnaissance in preparation for a larger expedition in 54 B.C., was his reason for making the invasion of 55 B.C. But though he does not state them explicitly, his ultimate intentions may be inferred. 'He knew the size of Britain with a fair degree of accuracy; he knew that its inhabitants were less civilised and less highly organised both in politics and in war than the Gauls; he meant in the following year to invade the country with five legions and to keep them there for the winter; and when all these facts are considered at once, it can hardly be doubted that his plan was to conquer the whole island.' * Perhaps it was the frustration of his plans that made him conceal their existence.

The expedition of 55 B.C. hardly did more than secure a landing-place—and that a precarious one—on the coast of Kent. Nor was that of 54 B.C. fruitful in important results, though Caesar brought five

* Collingwood and Myres, *Roman Britain and the English Settlements*, p. 34.

legions as well as auxiliary troops and stayed two or three months in the country. He might have achieved more, but he was forced to curtail the expedition and postpone indefinitely any ideas of conquest which he had by alarming news of rebellion in Gaul.

(3) Gaul had appeared conquered, but the harsh exactions of the Romans led to discontent. There was a rising in the north during the winter of 54 B.C., which forms the subject of the second half of this book, and, although this was with difficulty put down during the summer of 53, it was followed in the next winter by a much more serious rising in Central Gaul, united and organised by the Arvernian chief, Vercingetorix, who proved an adversary worthy of Caesar's mettle. Unlike the first part of the Gallic wars which had been marked by pitched battles in the field, and unlike the invasions of Germany and Britain in which Caesar had had to contend mainly with guerilla tactics, the third phase was marked by long and desperate sieges—Avaricum, Gergovia, Alesia—the story of which forms one of the most thrilling portions of Caesar's narrative. Vercingetorix surrendered, however, at Alesia in 52 B.C., and after his capitulation the independence of Gaul was irretrievably lost. With a pacified Gaul behind him, Caesar might now have turned his attention to Britain with good prospect of success, but political events compelled his return to Italy, and the conquest of Britain was postponed for a century.

IV. The Commentaries

When amidst his many activities did Caesar find time to write the elaborate and detailed account of the conquest of Gaul which the seven books of his Commentaries contain? When was it published?

And for what purpose? He must have been making notes and collecting documents for the work from the very beginning of his campaigns, and some scholars have thought that he wrote the full account year by year as each campaign was over. It is more likely, however, that, down to the surrender of Vercingetorix in 52 B.C., he merely gathered together sources of information—copies of the reports which he sent to the senate after each campaign; accounts by his subordinates of the independent commissions on which he sent them; and personal notes made as he went along to help his memory. The defeat of Vercingetorix brought the wars practically to an end. Gaul was still not finally pacified, but the back of the resistance was broken, and the fall of Alesia had made the ultimate conquest of the country only a matter of time. It was now that Caesar decided to compose a connected narrative from his various sources. There were special reasons why he wished to delay no longer the publication of his account. His conquests had stirred the imagination of his fellow-citizens in Rome and all manner of rumours were in circulation, put forward partly by his political enemies and partly by over-zealous friends. Caesar was anxious that the truth—or at any rate his own version of it—should be known, so that the rumours might be dispelled.

The Commentaries were designed primarily not as a literary work but as a political pamphlet, giving the authentic version of the Gallic campaigns for the glory of their author and the refutation of malicious gossipers and, indirectly, serving as material which future historians might use. It has been said that they 'stand midway between notes and finished history.' They were composed very rapidly: if scholars are right in believing that they were written in 52 B.C., we know from the course of events that they can have taken barely three months to write. A. Hirtius, friend and admirer of Caesar, who added an eighth book in imitation of his master in order to complete the account, remarked on the ease and speed with which Caesar accomplished the work. The haste with which it was done has indeed left blemishes here and there (p. 76), but on the whole Caesar's style is a model of clear and precise expression. He writes simply and lets the facts speak for themselves. In his anxiety to make his narrative appear as impersonal as possible, he usually refers to himself in the third person as Caesar. There is a little affectation in this, no doubt—a slight exaggeration of the impersonal nature of his narrative (he had the temperament of a man of action, fully conscious that his exploits were impressive enough for their bare recital to bring him renown) but the style is a real reflection of the man—a soldier's style, as he himself said. It reveals the same precise and orderly mind as is seen in all that he did.

The Commentaries, then, were written as much for Caesar's contemporaries as for posterity. Politically Caesar was on the defensive at this time: he knew that he was being attacked in Rome and he wished to justify himself before public opinion. What, then, is the historical value of his account? How far can the information which it contains be accepted as a truthful record of events? There are really two questions involved: (1) How far, if at all, has Caesar deliberately suppressed the truth when it was unfavourable to himself? (2) How far has he given inexact information through sheer ignorance of the truth?

(1) The temptation to minimise mistakes and to gloss over defeats must have been very great, and there are distinct signs that Caesar was at times guilty of such misrepresentation. It was not so much that

the facts which he gives are inexact as that significant facts are omitted and the facts which are given are coloured. There are two examples at least in the chapters contained in this book: first, his failure to state what his real intention about Britain was leaves it ambiguous whether his expeditions had succeeded in their object or not (pp. 73 and 95); and, secondly, his silence about a visit to the Kentish coast at a critical point during the expedition has the effect of minimising the seriousness of a very dangerous situation (p. 93). All this, of course, is easily explained if we remember that Caesar was writing an account of his exploits to vindicate himself, without pretending that what he wrote was the last word that would be said on the subject. He was probably no more guilty of misrepresentation than anyone else who has written his Memoires—and that is all one can expect.

(2) The second question is difficult because Caesar is our only authority for so much of what he writes. On the whole, however, where it is possible to check his information, the judgment of scholars confirms the general accuracy of Caesar's account, except in one respect. This exception concerns his topographical and geographical information, which can be shown very often to be inaccurate. It is significant that Caesar's port of embarkation in Gaul, his place of landing in Britain, and the ford by which he crossed the Thames are all disputed. His account of Britain falls far short of the best knowledge of his time. He was not interested in geography, and his three chapters on Britain, like other geographical digressions, were possibly put together by a secretary to give a little information to his readers about a country of which they had all heard but few knew anything definite. The vagueness of his descriptions, as in his references

to the winter-quarters of his legions during the winter of 54 B.C., have been the cause of much controversy. It is perhaps more in this respect than in any other that Caesar's work shows up as an improvisation to meet the needs of the moment.

V. Caesar's Legions

Caesar's army was composed of legions, each of a nominal strength of 6000 men (possibly 5000 was in practice the normal number), and of auxiliary troops (see note on ch. v, line 2). The legionaries were Roman citizens who had enlisted as volunteers, normally for twenty years, while the auxiliaries were drawn from peoples whom Rome had conquered. The diagram (p. 22) shows how the legion was organised. It was composed of ten cohorts, each with six centuries, and for certain purposes two centuries were grouped together to form a maniple. The rôle played by each of these subdivisions was as follows:

(i) The cohort was primarily a tactical unit. In the early days of Rome, the whole legion had fought in a solid phalanx, but during the fourth century B.C. the phalanx proved too rigid and unwieldy and gave way to an organisation by maniples of roughly 200 men each. The legion now fought in three lines, with ten maniples in each, so arranged that a space was left between one maniple and the next equal to the frontage of a maniple. This organisation proved eminently successful during the second century B.C. against enemies like the Macedonians who still fought in the solid phalanx, but when at the end of the century Rome came to deal with comparatively uncivilised tribes whose tactics were to 'stake everything upon a vigorous onslaught at the start of the battle,' * the maniples proved too

* Parker, *The Roman Legions*, p. 27.

small and the lines, with their gaps, too weak. Hence the cohort was substituted as the tactical unit. A

CENTURIES

COHORTS	1	2	3	4	5	6
I	*Primus Pilus*	*Pilus Posterior*	*Princeps Prior*	*Princeps Posterior*	*Hastatus Prior*	*Hastatus Posterior*
II	*Pilus Prior*	”	”	”	”	”
III	”	”	”	”	”	”
IV	”	”	”	”	”	”
V	”	”	”	”	”	”
VI	”	”	”	”	”	”
VII	”	”	”	”	”	”
VIII	”	”	”	”	”	”
IX	”	”	”	”	”	”
X	”	”	”	”	”	”
	1		2		3	

MANIPLES

Diagram illustrating the organisation of a legion. The names indicate the ranks of the centurions.

body of 600 men is large enough to have weight and resistance, and yet it is not too large to manoeuvre quickly. Thus the effect of the change was to give the lines greater stability without seriously diminishing their power of rapid movement. The triple line (*triplex acies*) continued to be the normal formation —with four cohorts in the front line and three in each of the others—but Caesar also used the double and single line if the need of keeping a reserve was not so urgent.

(ii) The century was a disciplinary unit. A hundred men is a convenient number for effective handling by a single commander, and it was largely on the centurions—commanders of the centuries— that Caesar relied for the efficient discipline of his troops. They had all risen from the ranks, and many of them were veterans who had voluntarily stayed on after the completion of their full term of service. The strictness of their discipline was proverbial, and they had the right of flogging and carried a rod as the symbol of their office (Pl. VII). Their ranks can be seen in the diagram (p. 22). Promotion seems to have been possible in two directions, first, from *hastatus posterior* to *pilus prior* in each cohort, and, secondly, from the tenth to the first cohort of the legion. The *pilus prior* of the first cohort was known as *primus pilus*: he was the senior centurion of the legion and under his care the legionary standard was placed.

(iii) To mark its identity and to foster and focus esprit de corps among its members, each legion had an *aquila*—a silver eagle carried on a long pole with various other decorations—which was a sacred emblem of its life-force, was preserved in a little shrine, and, if lost, involved the utmost disgrace. Besides the *aquila*, however, there were other standards, less important and less venerated, but serving a useful purpose in battle. There were the *signa*, of which (though their precise significance has caused much discussion) there seems to have been one to each maniple. If the legion became disorganised or was attacked while unprepared, it was desirable that the men should have a rallying-point, and the *signa* served this purpose. To have given one to each century would have involved having too many and caused confusion, while one to each cohort was too few. Hence the maniple which was little more than a historic survival seems to have been retained as a convenient unit between the two.

Before Caesar's time, the legionary officers were the military tribunes, of whom there were six to each legion. The character of this office, however, was changing. It had come to be held, not by tried soldiers but by young aristocrats who regarded it as an early step in their political career and as a means of gaining military experience. Such men were unsuitable for serious commands, and there is no instance of a tribune commanding a legion in action in the Gallic war. Caesar was in the habit of entrusting his legions to *legati*. The number of these officers varied with the rank of the governor and the special circumstances of the province; Caesar in Gaul had ten. Theoretically they were appointed by the senate, but in practice the wishes of the governor were consulted and he generally gave the posts to friends or relatives. Thus the *legati* in Gaul were not professional soldiers; they were Roman nobles and political friends of Caesar and, though able and competent subordinates, they do not seem to have been possessed of outstanding military skill. (We may well believe that the success which attended their efforts was largely due to the sound work of the centurions.) In spite of this, however, the experience gained in the use of *legati* during these years led in subsequent centuries to their permanent adoption as commanders of the legions.

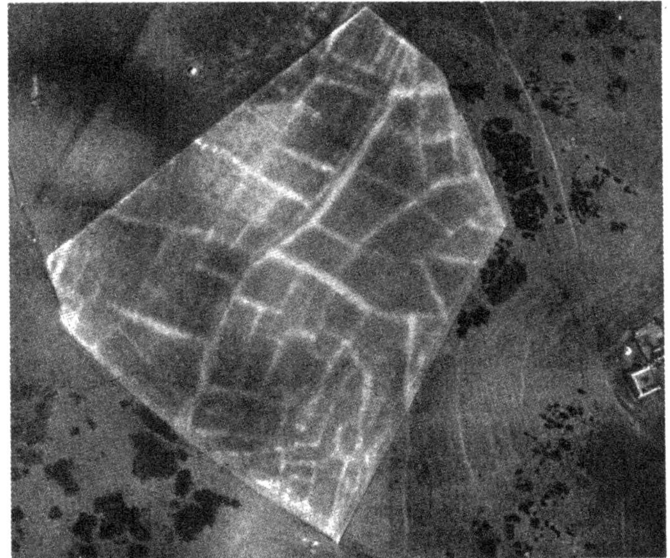

(*a*) Coombe Down, Wilts: the boundaries of the ancient fields, forming a network of banks, show as white lines where the top-soil is now thinner and the crops parched. Note the road or ditch (dark) between banks (light) running down the middle.

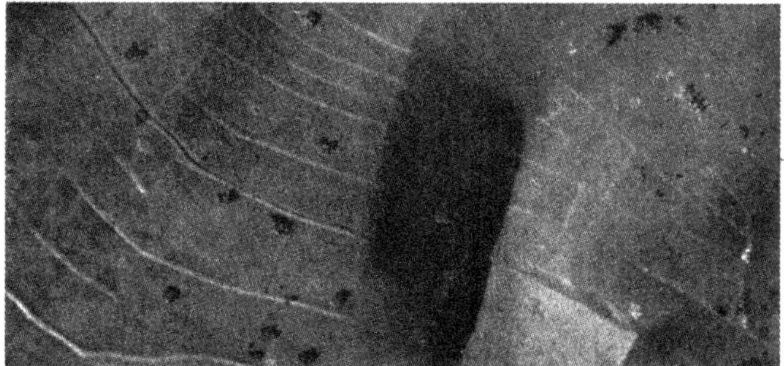

(*b*) Windover Hill, Eastbourne: cultivation-terraces on the slope, revealed by the sun's rays striking against their lower edge.

I. Celtic Fields revealed by Air-photography

II. (*a*) Iron Currency-Bars, found in S.-W. England: 11, 22, and 44 oz. respectively. Probably represent a form of currency used before coinage proper was introduced (p. 86). Note the rudely shaped handles.

II. (*b*) Coins used in Celtic Britain. (i) Gold (*c.* 75 B.C.): types derived from coins of Philip of Macedon with head of Apollo on one side and chariot on the other; by a repeated process of unintelligent copying they have become degraded to meaningless dots and dashes (p. 86). (ii) Gold (*c.* 50 B.C.): current in Cassivellaunus' kingdom. A pattern divided by a wreath has replaced the head of Apollo, and on the back is a spirited horse. (iii) Gold (*c.* 30 B.C.): struck in Britain for Commius, whose name COMMIOS can be read to R. of the horse (p. 94). (iv) Silver (*c.* 60 B.C.): struck for the Aeduan chief, Dumnorix. DUBNOCOV on the face is unexplained; on the back is the name DUBNOREX and a warrior holding a whip and severed head.

(*a*) Shield of polished bronze found in the Thames at Battersea: early first century B.C.; 30 inches long. The embossed design is ornamented with discs of red enamel enclosing a swastika.

(i)

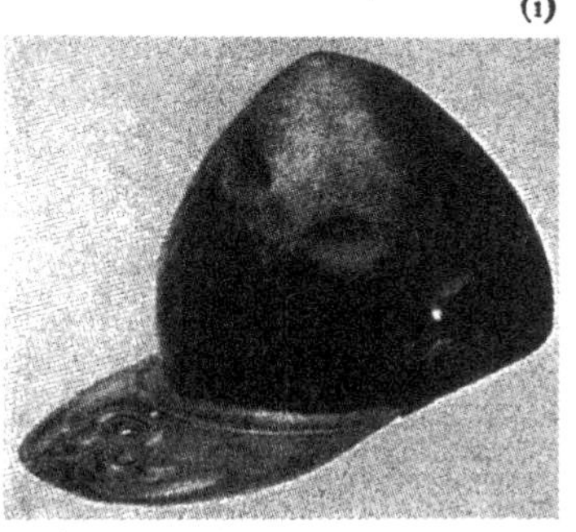

(ii)

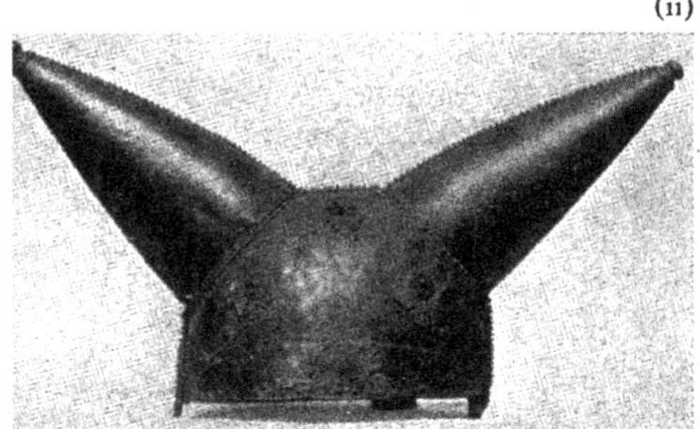

(*b*) Bronze helmets: (i) found in N. England. Rivet-holes show that there was a knob at the top. There were probably cheek-pieces. Note the broad neck-guard, with enamelled and embossed design. (ii) found in the Thames at Waterloo Bridge. Has no knob or neck-guard; fastened by a chin-strap; enamelled and embossed ornament.

III. Celtic Armour of British Workmanship

IV. CHARIOT-BURIAL, SOMME BIONNE, MARNE. The chariot was placed in a grave 9½ feet long, 6 feet wide, and nearly 4 feet deep. The wooden parts, which lay on the floor of the grave, have perished. Trenches were sunk to hold the wheels (the metal tires and hoops can be seen). The body rested on the axle and pole, and the latter protruded through a channel leading to a trench for the yoke. Here are the bridle-bits and trappings (for breast-harness and head-stall) of two horses. The position of the body implies that the chariot was open in front.

V. JULIUS CAESAR. Sculptured portraits of Caesar are few. Though cold and uninspired in workmanship, this probably represents more nearly than any other work of art Caesar's features at the height of his power. From the ancient biographer, Suetonius, we learn that he was of good stature and fair skinned, with shapely limbs, rather full mouth, and black, lively eyes, and that he brushed his hair forward from the crown to hide its thinness in front, and, for the same reason, he preferred best of all his honours the right of wearing a laurel crown. On coins he is represented as haggard and thin.

VI. Trophy of Roman Armour. A trophy, erected on the field of battle after a victory, consisted originally of a tree-trunk on which were hung spoils taken from the enemy. This trophy, made from models of Roman armour, gives an idea of the equipment of a legionary: woollen tunic reaching almost to his knees; over it a leather cuirass, fastened by a belt, with metal plates and sporran; cloak (used also as a blanket); helmet with cheek-pieces and neck-guard (the crest, if worn, was donned only on the eve of an engagement); leather shield, strengthened by metal rim and boss; sword (to L.), about 2 feet long and two-edged; dagger (to R.); two javelins (*pila*), about 7 feet long.

VII. Tombstone of Centurion killed in Germany in A.D. 9. The deceased is represented with metal (?) cuirass, with a tunic of strips of leather (?). Over the cuirass is a frame, with embossed metal plaques (*phalerae*); two ornamental rings hang at his neck (*torques*); and he wears armlets—all three the rewards of distinguished service. He wears a crown of oak leaves, the highest reward for individual acts of valour. On his left arm and shoulder he carries his cloak, and in his right hand holds the rod which was the mark of his rank (p. 23).

(*a*) The prow of a bireme being rowed into action. The name is believed to come from the number of rowers that sat at each oar or on each bench. Two banks of oars are visible. Over the rowers' heads is a deck, on which stand troops, and nearby is a wooden turret for their protection.

(*b*) A merchant vessel of a type used on rivers. On the prow is the head of a dragon, and, below the gunwale, an eye; at the stern is a Roman wolf. The helmsman steers with a large oar (possibly one on each side), while the coxwain gives the time to the rowers by clapping his hands. The cargo—barrels of wine—is piled down the centre. The rowers are represented facing the way they are going.

VIII. Roman Ships

IX. AIR-PHOTOGRAPH OF DEAL, KENT, looking N. to Pegwell Bay, and showing the gently sloping beach which tempted Caesar to land in this region (p. 81). The site of his naval camp was probably to the S., being now covered by houses. The Isle of Thanet is visible at the top and, just below it, the course and mouth of the River Stour, where in ancient times lay an island (now Richborough).

(*a*) Cutting through the inner bank of the Devil's Dyke, Wheathampstead, Herts (p. 92). The fortification consisted at this point of a huge ditch, bounded by banks; dated to the first half of the first century B.C.; probably the head-quarters of Cassivellaunus in 54 B.C.

(*b*) 'Beech-Bottom' Boundary-Dyke, near Wheathampstead and St. Albans. Contemporary with (*a*); political boundary between the Belgae and their Celtic neighbours and obstacle to cattle-raiding. Photograph taken from inside the ditch, showing N. slope, with men marking foot, middle, and top.

X. Belgic Fortifications in Britain

XII. The Country of the Ardennes. Ancient Gaul was much more densely wooded than modern France and Belgium (p. 3). This view of the R. Ourthe, near Le Héron, Belgium, where much forest still remains, gives an idea of the district in which the camps of Sabinus and Cotta and of Cicero were placed, and suggests the case with which a column on the march could be ambushed.

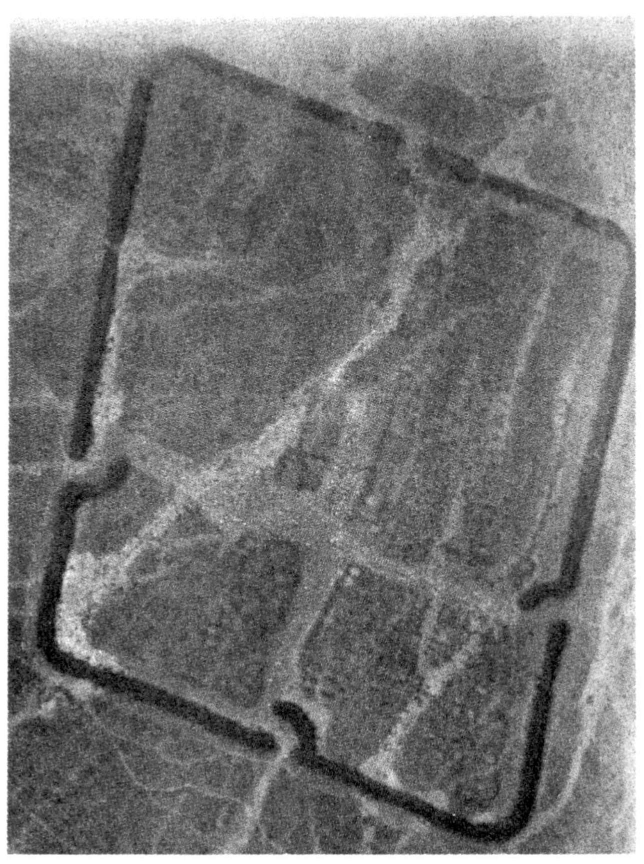

XI. Roman Camp at Masada. The arrangements of a Roman camp varied from time to time and even the shape, which was normally oblong, might be altered to suit the terrain. Actual photographs are difficult to obtain owing to the scantiness of the remains. The illustration shows a semi-permanent camp of the second century A.D. from Masada in Palestine, as revealed by air-photography. Though the camp is not rectangular in shape, the layout of the rampart, gates, main axes, central forum, head-quarters, and hutments follows the standard pattern (p. 97).

CAESAR'S GALLIC WAR
BOOK V

NOTE

The fifth book of the Commentaries deals with two main subjects: (A) chs. I–XXIV: the second invasion of Britain; (B) chs. XXV–LVIII: the revolt in north Gaul during the following winter. Attacks are described on the winter quarters of three separate legions, viz. (i) that of Q. Titurius Sabinus and L. Aurunculeius Cotta (chs. XXVI–XXXVII); (ii) that of Q. Cicero (chs. XXXVIII–LII); (iii) that of T. Labienus (chs. LV–LVIII).

(A) THE SECOND INVASION OF BRITAIN

CHS. 1–7. *Plans were made for a more resolute invasion of Britain the following year. Caesar himself spent the winter in Cisalpine Gaul and Illyricum, but had a fleet built during his absence and, on his return, assembled it at Portus Itius. He smoothed over an incipient revolt among the Treveri, and decided to take certain lukewarm Gallic chieftains with him to Britain as hostages. One of these, named Dumnorix, who refused to accompany him and ran away, was killed.*

I

L. Domitio App. Claudio consulibus, discedens ab hibernis Caesar in Italiam, ut quotannis facere consuerat, legatis imperat quos legionibus praefecerat uti quam plurimas possent hieme navis aedificandas veteresque reficiendas curarent. Earum modum formamque demonstrat. Ad celeritatem onerandi subductionesque paulo facit humiliores quam quibus in nostro mari uti consuevimus, atque id eo magis quod propter crebras commutationes aestuum minus magnos ibi fluctus fieri cognoverat; ad onera, ad multitudinem iumentorum transportandam paulo latiores quam quibus in reliquis utimur maribus. Has omnis actuarias imperat fieri, quam ad rem multum humilitas adiuvat. Ea quae sunt usui ad armandas navis ex Hispania apportari iubet. Ipse, conventibus Galliae citerioris peractis, in Illyricum proficiscitur, quod a Pirustis finitimam partem provinciae incursionibus vastari audiebat. Eo cum venisset, civitatibus milites imperat certumque in locum convenire iubet. Qua re nuntiata Pirustae legatos ad eum mittunt qui doceant nihil earum rerum publico factum consilio; seseque paratos esse demonstrant omnibus rationibus de iniuriis satisfacere. Percepta oratione eorum, Caesar obsides imperat eosque ad certam diem adduci iubet; nisi ita fecerint, sese bello civitatem persecuturum demonstrat. Eis ad diem adductis, ut imperaverat, arbitros inter civitates dat qui litem aestiment poenamque constituant.

II

His confectis rebus conventibusque peractis, in citeriorem Galliam revertitur atque inde ad exercitum proficiscitur. Eo cum venisset, circuitis omnibus hibernis, singulari militum studio in summa omnium rerum inopia circiter sescentas eius generis cuius supra demonstravimus navis et longas XXVIII invenit instructas neque multum abesse ab eo quin paucis diebus deduci possint. Collaudatis militibus atque eis qui negotio praefuerant, quid fieri velit ostendit atque omnis ad portum Itium convenire iubet, quo ex portu commodissimum in Britanniam traiectum esse cognoverat, circiter milium passuum

XXX transmissum a continenti. Huic rei quod satis esse visum est militum reliquit: ipse cum legionibus expeditis IIII et equitibus DCCC in fines Treverorum proficiscitur, quod hi neque ad concilia veniebant neque imperio parebant Germanosque Transrhenanos sollicitare dicebantur.

III

Haec civitas longe plurimum totius Galliae equitatu valet magnasque habet copias peditum Rhenumque, ut supra demonstravimus, tangit. In ea civitate duo de principatu inter se contendebant, Indutiomarus et Cingetorix: e quibus alter, simul atque de Caesaris legionumque adventu cognitum est, ad eum venit, se suosque omnis in officio futuros neque ab amicitia populi Romani defecturos confirmavit, quaeque in Treveris gererentur ostendit. At Indutiomarus equitatum peditatumque cogere, eisque qui per aetatem in armis esse non poterant in silvam Arduennam abditis, quae ingenti magnitudine per medios finis Treverorum a flumine Rheno ad initium Remorum pertinet, bellum parare instituit. Sed postea quam non nulli principes ex ea civitate et familiaritate Cingetorigis adducti et adventu nostri exercitus perterriti ad Caesarem venerunt et de suis privatim rebus ab eo petere coeperunt, quoniam civitati consulere non possent, veritus ne ab omnibus desereretur Indutiomarus legatos ad Caesarem mittit: sese idcirco ab suis discedere atque ad eum venire noluisse quo facilius civitatem in officio contineret, ne omnis nobilitatis discessu plebs propter imprudentiam laberetur. Itaque esse civitatem in sua potestate seque, si Caesar permitteret, ad eum in castra venturum, suas civitatisque fortunas eius fidei permissurum.

IV

Caesar, etsi intellegebat qua de causa ea dicerentur quaeque eum res ab instituto consilio deterreret, tamen, ne aestatem in Treveris consumere cogeretur omnibus ad Britannicum bellum rebus comparatis, Indutiomarum ad se cum ducentis obsidibus venire iussit. His adductis, in eis filio propinquisque eius omnibus quos nominatim evocaverat, consolatus Indutiomarum hortatusque est uti in officio maneret; nihilo tamen setius principibus Treverorum ad se convocatis hos singillatim Cingetorigi conciliavit: quod cum merito eius a se fieri intellegebat, tum magni interesse arbitrabatur eius auctoritatem inter suos quam plurimum valere, cuius tam egregiam in se voluntatem perspexisset. Id tulit factum graviter Indutiomarus, suam gratiam inter suos minui, et qui iam ante inimico in nos animo fuisset multo gravius hoc dolore exarsit.

V

His rebus constitutis, Caesar ad portum Itium cum legionibus pervenit. Ibi cognoscit LX navis, quae in Meldis factae erant, tempestate reiectas cursum tenere non potuisse atque eodem unde erant profectae revertisse: reliquas paratas ad navigandum atque omnibus rebus instructas invenit. Eodem equitatus totius Galliae convenit, numero milium quattuor, principesque ex omnibus civitatibus; ex quibus perpaucos, quorum in se fidem perspexerat relinquere in Gallia, reliquos obsidum loco secum ducere decreverat, quod, cum ipse abesset, motum Galliae verebatur.

VI

Erat una cum ceteris Dumnorix Aeduus, de quo ante ab nobis dictum est. Hunc secum habere in primis constituerat, quod eum cupidum rerum novarum, cupidum imperi, magni animi, magnae inter Gallos auctoritatis cognoverat. Accedebat huc quod in concilio Aeduorum Dumnorix dixerat sibi a Caesare regnum civitatis deferri; quod dictum Aedui graviter ferebant, neque recusandi aut deprecandi causa legatos ad Caesarem mittere audebant. Id factum ex suis hospitibus Caesar cognoverat. Ille omnibus primo precibus petere contendit ut in Gallia relinqueretur, partim quod insuetus navigandi mare timeret, partim quod religionibus impediri sese diceret. Postea quam id obstinate sibi negari vidit, omni spe impetrandi adempta, principes Galliae sollicitare, sevocare singulos hortarique coepit uti in continenti remanerent; metu territare: non sine causa fieri ut Gallia omni nobilitate spoliaretur; id esse consilium Caesaris ut quos in conspectu Galliae interficere vereretur hos omnes in Britanniam traductos necaret; fidem reliquis interponere, ius iurandum poscere ut quod esse ex usu Galliae intellexissent communi consilio administrarent. Haec a compluribus ad Caesarem deferebantur.

VII

Qua re cognita Caesar, quod tantum civitati Aeduae dignitatis tribuebat, coercendum atque deterrendum quibuscumque rebus posset Dumnorigem statuebat; quod longius eius amentiam progredi videbat, prospiciendum, ne quid sibi ac rei publicae nocere posset. Itaque dies circiter XXV in eo loco commoratus, quod Caurus ventus navigationem impediebat, qui magnam partem omnis temporis in eis locis flare consuevit, dabat operam ut in officio Dumnorigem contineret, nihilo tamen setius omnia eius consilia cognosceret; tandem idoneam nactus tempestatem milites equitesque conscendere in navis iubet. At omnium impeditis animis Dumnorix cum equitibus Aeduorum a castris insciente Caesare domum discedere coepit. Qua re nuntiata Caesar, intermissa profectione atque omnibus rebus postpositis, magnam partem equitatus ad eum insequendum mittit retrahique imperat; si vim faciat neque pareat, interfici iubet, nihil hunc se absente pro sano facturum arbitratus qui praesentis imperium neglexisset. Ille enim revocatus resistere ac se manu defendere suorumque fidem implorare coepit, saepe clamitans liberum se liberaeque esse civitatis. Illi, ut erat imperatum, circumsistunt hominem atque interficiunt: at equites Aedui ad Caesarem omnes revertuntur.

CHS. 8–9. *Leaving Labienus with a strong force to protect his base and to watch Gaul, Caesar crossed the Channel with five legions,* 2000 *Gallic cavalry, and a huge fleet. He disembarked at or near his landing-place of the year before, and, leaving his fleet at anchor and a force to protect it, he marched some twelve miles inland and stormed a hill-fortress in which the Britons had taken refuge.*

VIII

His rebus gestis, Labieno in continente cum tribus legionibus et equitum milibus duobus relicto ut portus tueretur et rem frumentariam provideret quaeque in Gallia gererentur cognosceret consiliumque pro tempore et pro re caperet, ipse cum quinque legionibus et pari numero equitum, quem in continenti reliquerat, ad solis occasum navis solvit et leni Africo provectus media circiter nocte vento intermisso cursum non tenuit, et longius delatus aestu orta luce sub sinistra Britanniam relictam conspexit. Tum rursus aestus commutationem secutus remis contendit ut eam partem insulae caperet qua optimum esse egressum superiore aestate cognoverat. Qua in re admodum fuit militum virtus laudanda, qui vectoriis gravibusque navigiis non intermisso remigandi labore longarum navium cursum adaequarunt. Accessum est ad Britanniam omnibus navibus meridiano fere tempore, neque in eo loco hostis est visus; sed, ut postea Caesar ex captivis cognovit, cum magnae manus eo convenissent, multitudine navium perterritae, quae cum annotinis privatisque quas sui quisque commodi fecerat amplius octingentae uno erant visae tempore, a litore discesserant ac se in superiora loca abdiderant.

IX

Caesar, exposito exercitu et loco castris idoneo capto, ubi ex captivis cognovit quo in loco hostium copiae consedissent, cohortibus decem ad mare relictis et equitibus trecentis qui praesidio navibus essent, de tertia vigilia ad hostis contendit, eo minus veritus navibus quod in litore molli atque aperto deligatas ad ancoram relinquebat, et praesidio navibus Q. Atrium praefecit. Ipse noctu progressus milia passuum circiter XII hostium copias conspicatus est. Illi equitatu atque essedis ad flumen progressi ex loco superiore nostros prohibere et proelium committere coeperunt. Repulsi ab equitatu se in silvas abdiderunt, locum nacti egregie et natura et opere munitum, quem domestici belli, ut videbatur, causa iam ante praeparaverant; nam crebris arboribus succisis omnes introitus erant praeclusi. Ipsi ex silvis rari propugnabant nostrosque intra munitiones ingredi prohibebant. At milites legionis septimae, testudine facta et aggere ad munitiones adiecto, locum ceperunt eosque ex silvis expulerunt paucis vulneribus acceptis. Sed eos fugientis longius Caesar prosequi vetuit, et quod loci naturam ignorabat et quod magna parte diei consumpta munitioni castrorum tempus relinqui volebat.

CHS. 10–11. *Next day flying columns had set out in pursuit of the defeated Britons, when news arrived that the fleet had been seriously damaged by a storm. The pursuit was called off, and Caesar hastened back to the shore, where he spent ten days in having the ships drawn up above high-water mark and entrenched with his camp in a single fortification. This disaster, like that of the previous year, led to renewed hostility on the part of the Britons, who appointed Cassivellaunus their commander-in-chief.*

X

Postridie eius diei mane tripertito milites equitesque in expeditionem misit, ut eos qui fugerant persequerentur. His aliquantum itineris progressis, cum iam extremi essent in prospectu, equites a Q. Atrio ad Caesarem venerunt qui nuntiarent superiore nocte maxima coorta tempestate prope omnis navis adflictas atque in litore eiectas esse, quod neque ancorae funesque subsisterent neque nautae gubernatoresque vim tempestatis pati possent; itaque ex eo concursu navium magnum esse incommodum acceptum.

XI

His rebus cognitis, Caesar legiones equitatumque revocari atque in itinere resistere iubet, ipse ad navis revertitur: eadem fere quae ex nuntiis litterisque cognoverat coram perspicit, sic ut amissis circiter XL navibus reliquae tamen refici posse magno negotio viderentur. Itaque ex legionibus fabros deligit et ex continenti alios arcessi iubet; Labieno scribit ut quam plurimas posset eis legionibus, quae sunt apud eum, navis instituat. Ipse, etsi res erat multae operae ac laboris, tamen commodissimum esse statuit omnis navis subduci et cum castris una munitione coniungi. In his rebus circiter dies X consumit, ne nocturnis quidem temporibus ad laborem militum intermissis. Subductis navibus castrisque egregie munitis, easdem copias, quas ante, praesidio navibus reliquit: ipse eodem unde redierat proficiscitur. Eo cum venisset, maiores iam undique in eum locum copiae Britannorum convenerant summa imperi bellique administrandi communi consilio permissa Cassivellauno, cuius finis a maritimis civitatibus flumen dividit quod appellatur Tamesis a mari circiter milia passuum LXXX. Huic superiore tempore cum reliquis civitatibus continentia bella intercesserant; sed nostro adventu permoti Britanni hunc toti bello imperioque praefecerant.

CHS. 12–14. *In parenthesis, Caesar describes the resources of Britain, its shape and size, and certain manners and customs of its inhabitants.*

XII

Britanniae pars interior ab eis incolitur quos natos in insula ipsi memoria proditum dicunt, maritima pars ab eis qui praedae ac belli inferendi causa ex Belgio transierant, qui omnes fere eis nominibus civitatum appellantur quibus orti ex civitatibus eo pervenerunt, et bello inlato ibi permanserunt atque agros colere coeperunt. Hominum est infinita multitudo creberrimaque aedificia fere Gallicis consimilia, pecorum magnus numerus. Utuntur aut aere aut nummo aureo aut taleis ferreis ad certum pondus examinatis pro nummo. Nascitur ibi plumbum album in mediterraneis regionibus, in maritimis ferrum, sed eius exigua est copia; aere utuntur importato. Materia cuiusque generis ut in Gallia est, praeter fagum atque abietem. Leporem et gallinam et anserem gustare fas non putant; haec tamen alunt animi voluptatisque causa. Loca sunt temperatiora quam in Gallia, remissioribus frigoribus.

XIII

Insula natura triquetra, cuius unum latus est contra Galliam. Huius lateris alter angulus, qui est ad Cantium, quo fere omnes ex Gallia naves appelluntur, ad orientem solem, inferior ad meridiem spectat. Hoc pertinet circiter milia passuum quingenta. Alterum vergit ad Hispaniam atque occidentem solem; qua ex parte est Hibernia, dimidio minor, ut existimatur, quam Britannia, sed pari spatio transmissus atque ex Gallia est in Britanniam. In hoc medio cursu est insula quae appellatur Mona: complures praeterea minores subiectae insulae existimantur, de quibus insulis non nulli scripserunt dies continuos xxx sub bruma esse noctem. Nos nihil de eo percontationibus reperiebamus nisi certis ex aqua mensuris breviores esse quam in continenti noctes videbamus. Huius est longitudo lateris, ut fert illorum opinio, septingentorum milium. Tertium est contra septentriones, cui parti nulla est obiecta terra; sed eius angulus lateris maxime ad Germaniam spectat. Hoc milia passuum octingenta in longitudinem esse existimatur. Ita omnis insula est in circuitu vicies centum milium passuum.

XIV

Ex eis omnibus longe sunt humanissimi qui Cantium incolunt, quae regio est maritima omnis, neque multum a Gallica differunt consuetudine. Interiores plerique frumenta non serunt, sed lacte et carne vivunt pellibusque sunt vestiti. Omnes vero se Britanni vitro inficiunt, quod caeruleum efficit colorem, atque hoc horridiores sunt in pugna aspectu; capilloque sunt promisso atque omni parte corporis rasa, praeter caput et labrum superius. Uxores habent deni duodenique inter se communis, et maxime frates cum fratribus parentesque cum liberis; sed qui sunt ex eis nati eorum habentur liberi quo primum virgo quaeque deducta est.

CHS. 15–17. *When Caesar resumed his advance, he found the Britons, now well led by a single commander, much more difficult to deal with. They harassed his line of march and, at nightfall, attacked the troops which he had thrown out as a screen while his legions were fortifying a camp. As this engagement took place within his view, Caesar was able to observe the tactical use which the Britons made of their war-chariots. Next day they attacked the Roman foragers, but Caesar drove them off, and this defeat caused them to disperse so that they never met the Romans in full force again.*

XV

Equites hostium essedariique acriter proelio cum equitatu nostro in itinere conflixerunt, tamen ut nostri omnibus partibus superiores fuerint atque eos in silvas collisque compulerint: sed compluribus interfectis cupidius insecuti non nullos ex suis amiserunt. At illi, intermisso spatio, imprudentibus nostris atque occupatis in munitione castrorum, subito se ex silvis eiecerunt, impetuque in eos facto qui erant in statione pro castris collocati, acriter pugnaverunt; duabusque missis subsidio cohortibus a Caesare, atque eis primis legionum duarum, cum haec perexiguo intermisso loci spatio inter se constitissent, novo genere pugnae perterritis nostris, per medios audacissime perruperunt seque inde incolumes receperunt. Eo die Q. Laberius Durus, tribunus militum, interficitur. Illi pluribus summissis cohortibus repelluntur.

XVI

Toto hoc in genere pugnae, cum sub oculis omnium ac pro castris dimicaretur, intellectum est nostros propter gravitatem armorum, quod neque insequi cedentis possent neque ab signis discedere auderent, minus aptos esse ad huius generis hostem, equites autem magno cum periculo proelio dimicare propterea quod illi etiam consulto plerumque cederent et, cum paulum ab legionibus nostros removissent, ex essedis desilirent et pedibus dispari proelio contenderent. Equestris autem proeli ratio et cedentibus et insequentibus par atque idem periculum inferebat. Accedebat huc ut numquam conferti sed rari magnisque intervallis proeliarentur stationesque dispositas haberent, atque alios alii deinceps exciperent integrique et recentes defatigatis succederent.

XVII

Postero die procul a castris hostes in collibus constiterunt, rarique se ostendere et lenius quam pridie nostros equites proelio lacessere coeperunt. Sed meridie, cum Caesar pabulandi causa tris legiones atque omnem equitatum cum C. Trebonio legato misisset, repente ex omnibus partibus ad pabulatores advolaverunt, sic uti ab signis legionibusque non absisterent. Nostri acriter in eos impetu facto reppulerunt neque finem sequendi fecerunt, quoad subsidio confisi equites, cum post se legiones viderent, praecipites hostis egerunt, magnoque eorum numero interfecto, neque sui colligendi neque consistendi aut ex essedis desiliendi facultatem dederunt. Ex hac fuga protinus quae undique convenerant auxilia discesserunt, neque post id tempus umquam summis nobiscum copiis hostes contenderunt.

CHS. 18–20. *Caesar resolved to strike at Cassivellaunus' own territory. He forced the passage of the Thames, and, though harried all along his march by Cassivellaunus, who drove the population away from the advancing troops and severely restricted the Roman foraging-parties, he received the submission of Cassivellaunus' neighbour and long-standing enemy, the Trinobantes. From them he got the provisions which he had been unable to obtain on the march.*

XVIII

Caesar, cognito consilio eorum, ad flumen Tamesim in finis Cassivellauni exercitum duxit; quod flumen uno omnino loco pedibus, atque hoc aegre, transiri potest. Eo cum venisset, animum advertit ad alteram fluminis ripam magnas esse copias hostium instructas. Ripa autem erat acutis sudibus praefixisque munita, eiusdemque generis sub aqua defixae sudes flumine tegebantur. Eis rebus cognitis a captivis perfugisque, Caesar praemisso equitatu confestim legiones subsequi iussit. Sed ea celeritate atque eo impetu milites ierunt, cum capite solo ex aqua exstarent, ut hostes impetum legionum atque equitum sustinere non possent ripasque dimitterent ac se fugae mandarent.

XIX

Cassivellaunus, ut supra demonstravimus, omni deposita spe contentionis, dimissis amplioribus copiis, milibus circiter quattuor essedariorum relictis, itinera nostra servabat paulumque ex via excedebat locisque impeditis ac silvestribus sese occultabat, atque eis regionibus quibus nos iter facturos cognoverat pecora atque homines ex agris in silvas compellebat et, cum equitatus noster liberius praedandi vastandique causa se in agros eiecerat, omnibus viis semitisque essedarios ex silvis emittebat et magno cum periculo nostrorum equitum cum eis confligebat atque hoc metu latius vagari prohibebat. Relinquebatur ut neque longius ab agmine legionum discedi Caesar pateretur, et tantum in agris vastandis incendiisque faciendis hostibus noceretur, quantum labore atque itinere legionarii milites efficere poterant.

XX

Interim Trinobantes, prope firmissima earum regionum civitas, ex qua Mandubracius adulescens Caesaris fidem secutus ad eum in continentem Galliam venerat, cuius pater in ea civitate regnum obtinuerat interfectusque erat a Cassivellauno, ipse fuga mortem vitaverat, legatos ad Caesarem mittunt pollicenturque sese ei dedituros atque imperata facturos: petunt ut Mandubracium ab iniuria Cassivellauni defendat atque in civitatem mittat qui praesit imperiumque obtineat. Eis Caesar imperat obsides XL frumentumque exercitui, Mandubraciumque ad eos mittit. Illi imperata celeriter fecerunt, obsides ad numerum frumentumque miserunt.

CHS. 21–23. *Five other tribes submitted and revealed to Caesar the whereabouts of Cassivellaunus' capital. He stormed and captured it, inflicting great losses on the enemy and getting hold of much live stock. To distract Caesar's attention, Cassivellaunus persuaded four Kentish kings to attack the naval camp on the Kentish coast. But, when this attack failed, Cassivellaunus made peace through the mediation of Commius. He was required to refrain from attacks on the Trinobantes, while the Britons as a whole were asked to furnish hostages and an annual tribute. Anxious at the disturbed state of Gaul, Caesar re-crossed the Channel without delay.*

XXI

Trinobantibus defensis atque ab omni militum iniuria prohibitis, Cenimagni, Segontiaci, Ancalites, Bibroci, Cassi legationibus missis sese Caesari dedunt. Ab eis cognoscit non longe ex eo loco oppidum Cassivellauni abesse silvis paludibusque munitum, quo satis magnus hominum pecorisque numerus convenerit. Oppidum autem Britanni vocant, cum silvas impeditas vallo atque fossa munierunt, quo incursionis hostium vitandae causa convenire consuerunt. Eo proficiscitur cum legionibus: locum reperit egregie natura atque opere munitum: tamen hunc duabus ex partibus oppugnare contendit. Hostes paulisper morati militum nostrorum impetum non tulerunt seseque alia ex parte oppidi eiecerunt. Magnus ibi numerus pecoris repertus, multique in fuga sunt comprehensi atque interfecti.

XXII

Dum haec in eis locis geruntur, Cassivellaunus ad Cantium, quod esse ad mare supra demonstravimus, quibus regionibus quattuor reges praeerant, Cingetorix, Carvilius, Taximagulus, Segovax, nuntios mittit atque eis imperat uti coactis omnibus copiis castra navalia de improviso adoriantur atque oppugnent. Ei cum ad castra venissent, nostri eruptione facta, multis eorum interfectis, capto etiam nobili duce Lugotorige, suos incolumes reduxerunt. Cassivellaunus, hoc proelio nuntiato, tot detrimentis acceptis, vastatis finibus, maxime etiam permotus defectione civitatum legatos per Atrebatem Commium de deditione ad Caesarem mittit. Caesar, cum constituisset hiemare in continenti propter repentinos Galliae motus neque multum aestatis superesset atque id facile extrahi posse intellegeret, obsides imperat et quid in annos singulos vectigalis populo Romano Britannia penderet constituit; interdicit atque imperat Cassivellauno ne Mandubracio neu Trinobantibus noceat.

XXIII

Obsidibus acceptis, exercitum reducit ad mare, navis invenit refectas. Eis deductis, quod et captivorum magnum numerum habebat et non nullae tempestate deperierant naves, duobus commeatibus exercitum reportare instituit. Ac sic accidit uti ex tanto navium numero tot navigationibus neque hoc neque superiore anno ulla omnino navis, quae milites portaret, desideraretur; at ex eis quae inanes ex continenti ad eum remitterentur, et prioris commeatus expositis militibus, et quas postea

Labienus faciendas curaverat numero LX, perpaucae locum caperent, reliquae fere omnes reicerentur. Quas cum aliquamdiu Caesar frustra exspectasset, ne anni tempore a navigatione excluderetur, quod aequinoctium suberat, necessario angustius milites collocavit ac summa tranquillitate consecuta, secunda inita cum solvisset vigilia, prima luce terram attigit omnisque incolumis navis perduxit.

(B) THE REVOLT IN GAUL

CHS. 24–25. *Owing to a drought and consequent shortage of food, Caesar was obliged to distribute his legions in winter quarters over a wider area than usual. He himself decided to stay in North Gaul until the legions were properly settled, and he had, in the event, to modify his dispositions somewhat in view of the murder of Tasgetius, king of the Carnutes.*

XXIV

Subductis navibus, concilioque Gallorum Samarobrivae peracto, quod eo anno frumentum in Gallia propter siccitates angustius provenerat, coactus est aliter ac superioribus annis exercitum in hibernis collocare, legionesque in pluris civitates distribuere. Ex quibus unam in Morinos ducendam C. Fabio legato dedit, alteram in Nervos Q. Ciceroni, tertiam in Esubios L. Roscio; quartam in Remis cum T. Labieno in confinio Treverorum hiemare iussit. Tris in † Belgis † collocavit: eis M. Crassum quaestorem et L. Munatium Plancum et C. Trebonium legatos praefecit. Unam legionem, quam proxime trans Padum conscripserat, et cohortis v in Eburones, quorum pars maxima est inter Mosam ac Rhenum, qui sub imperio Ambiorigis et Catuvolci erant, misit. Eis militibus Q. Titurium Sabinum et L. Aurunculeium Cottam legatos praeesse iussit. Ad hunc modum distributis legionibus, facillime inopiae frumentariae sese mederi posse existimavit. Atque harum tamen omnium legionum hiberna, praeter eam quam L. Roscio in pacatissimam et quietissimam partem ducendam dederat, milibus passuum centum continebantur. Ipse interea, quoad legiones collocatas munitaque hiberna cognovisset, in Gallia morari constituit.

XXV

Erat in Carnutibus summo loco natus Tasgetius, cuius maiores in sua civitate regnum obtinuerant. Huic Caesar pro eius virtute atque in se benevolentia, quod in omnibus bellis singulari eius opera fuerat usus, maiorum locum restituerat. Tertium iam hunc annum regnantem †inimicis iam multis palam ex civitate et eis auctoribus eum †interfecerunt. Defertur ea res ad Caesarem. Ille veritus, quod ad pluris pertinebat, ne civitas eorum impulsu deficeret, L. Plancum cum legione ex Belgio celeriter in Carnutes proficisci iubet ibique hiemare, quorumque opera cognoverat Tasgetium interfectum, hos comprehensos ad se mittere. Interim ab omnibus legatis quaestoribusque quibus legiones tradiderat certior factus est in hiberna perventum locumque hibernis esse munitum.

(i) The Attack on Sabinus and Cotta

Ch. 26. *A fortnight later there was a sudden revolt. It began amongst the Eburones, whose kings, Ambiorix and Catuvolcus, made an abortive attack on the camp of Sabinus and Cotta.*

XXVI

Diebus circiter quindecim quibus in hiberna ventum est initium repentini tumultus ac defectionis ortum est ab Ambiorige et Catuvolco; qui, cum ad finis regni sui Sabino Cottaeque praesto fuissent frumentumque in hiberna comportavissent, Indutiomari Treveri nuntiis impulsi suos concitaverunt subitoque oppressis lignatoribus magna manu ad castra oppugnatum venerunt. Cum celeriter nostri arma cepissent vallumque ascendissent atque una ex parte Hispanis equitibus emissis equestri proelio superiores fuissent, desperata re hostes suos ab oppugnatione reduxerunt. Tum suo more conclamaverunt, uti aliqui ex nostris ad colloquium prodiret: habere sese quae de re communi dicere vellent, quibus rebus controversias minui posse sperarent.

Chs. 27–31. *The Roman leaders sent out two representatives to confer with Ambiorix, who expressed gratitude to Caesar for former kindnesses but urged Sabinus, in view of the widespread nature of the revolt and the imminent arrival of reinforcements from Germany, to leave his winter quarters and take his troops either to Cicero or to Labienus. This advice was considered in a council of war. Opinions were divided, Sabinus being anxious to follow the Gaul's suggestion, while Cotta doubted his good faith. Cotta was finally overruled and the legion set out from the camp at daybreak.*

XXVII

Mittitur ad eos colloquendi causa C. Arpineius, eques Romanus, familiaris Q. Tituri, et Q. Iunius ex Hispania quidam, qui iam ante missu Caesaris ad Ambiorigem ventitare consuerat; apud quos Ambiorix ad hunc modum locutus est: sese pro Caesaris in se beneficiis plurimum ei confiteri debere, quod eius opera stipendio liberatus esset quod Aduatucis finitimis suis pendere consuesset, quodque ei et filius et fratris filius ab Caesare remissi essent, quos Aduatuci obsidum numero missos apud se in servitute et catenis tenuissent; neque id quod fecerit de oppugnatione castrorum aut iudicio aut voluntate sua fecisse sed coactu civitatis, suaque esse eiusmodi imperia ut non minus haberet iuris in se multitudo quam ipse in multitudinem. Civitati porro hanc fuisse belli causam, quod repentinae Gallorum coniurationi resistere non potuerit. Id se facile ex humilitate sua probare posse, quod non adeo sit imperitus rerum ut suis copiis populum Romanum superari posse confidat. Sed esse Galliae commune consilium: omnibus hibernis Caesaris oppugnandis hunc esse dictum diem, ne qua legio alterae legioni subsidio venire posset. Non facile Gallos Gallis negare potuisse, praesertim cum de reciperanda communi libertate consilium initum videretur. Quibus quoniam pro pietate satisfecerit, habere nunc se rationem offici pro beneficiis Caesaris: monere, orare Titurium pro hospitio ut suae ac militum saluti consulat. Magnam manum Germanorum conductam Rhenum transisse: hanc adfore biduo. Ipsorum esse consilium, velintne prius quam finitimi sentiant eductos ex hibernis milites aut ad Ciceronem aut ad Labienum deducere, quorum alter milia passuum circiter quinquaginta, alter paulo amplius ab eis absit. Illud se polliceri et iure iurando confirmare, tutum iter per finis daturum. Quod cum faciat, et civitati sese consulere, quod hibernis levetur, et Caesari pro eius meritis gratiam referre. Hac oratione habita discedit Ambiorix.

XXVIII

Arpineius at Iunius quae audierunt ad legatos deferunt. Illi repentina re perturbati, etsi ab hoste ea dicebantur, tamen non neglegenda existimabant, maximeque hac re permovebantur, quod civitatem ignobilem atque humilem Eburonum sua sponte populo Romano bellum facere ausam vix erat credendum. Itaque ad consilium rem deferunt magnaque inter eos exsistit controversia. L. Aurunculeius compluresque tribuni militum et primorum ordinum centuriones nihil temere agendum neque ex hibernis iniussu Caesaris discedendum existimabant; quantasvis magnas etiam copias Germanorum sustineri posse munitis hibernis docebant: rem esse testimonio, quod primum hostium impetum multis ultro vulneribus inlatis fortissime sustinuerint; re frumentaria non premi; interea et ex proximis hibernis et a Caesare conventura subsidia; postremo quid esset levius aut turpius quam auctore hoste de summis rebus capere consilium?

XXIX

Contra ea Titurius sero facturos clamitabat, cum maiores manus hostium adiunctis Germanis convenissent aut cum aliquid calamitatis in proximis hibernis esset acceptum. Brevem consulendi esse occasionem. Caesarem arbitrari profectum in Italiam; neque aliter Carnutes interficiendi Tasgeti consilium fuisse capturos neque Eburones, si ille adesset, tanta contemptione nostri ad castra venturos esse. Non hostem auctorem sed rem spectare: subesse Rhenum; magno esse Germanis dolori Ariovisti mortem et superiores nostras victorias; ardere Galliam tot contumeliis acceptis sub populi Romani imperium redactam, superiore gloria rei militaris exstincta. Postremo quis hoc sibi persuaderet, sine certa re Ambiorigem ad eiusmodi consilium descendisse? Suam senteniam in utramque partem esse tutam: si nihil esset durius, nullo cum periculo ad proximam legionem perventuros: si Gallia omnis cum Germanis consentiret, unam esse in celeritate positam salutem. Cottae quidem atque eorum qui dissentirent consilium quem haberet exitum, in quo si praesens periculum non, at certe longinqua obsidione fames esset timenda?

XXX

Hac in utramque partem disputatione habita, cum a Cotta primisque ordinibus acriter resisteretur, 'Vincite,' inquit, 'si ita vultis,' Sabinus, et id clariore voce, ut magna pars militum exaudiret: 'neque is sum,' inquit, 'qui gravissime ex vobis mortis periculo terrear: hi sapient; si gravius quid acciderit, abs te rationem reposcent qui, si per te liceat, perendino die cum proximis hibernis coniuncti communem cum reliquis belli casum sustineant, non reiecti et relegati longe ab ceteris aut ferro aut fame intereant.'

XXXI

Consurgitur ex consilio; comprehendunt utrumque et orant ne sua dissensione et pertinacia rem in summum periculum deducant: facilem esse rem, seu maneant, seu proficiscantur, si modo unum omnes sentiant ac probent; contra in dissensione nullam se salutem perspicere. Res disputatione ad mediam noctem perducitur. Tandem dat Cotta permotus manus: superat sententia Sabini. Pronuntiatur prima luce ituros. Consumitur vigiliis reliqua pars noctis, cum sua quisque miles circumspiceret, quid secum portare posset, quid ex instrumento hibernorum relinquere cogeretur. Omnia excogitantur, quare nec sine periculo maneatur et languore militum et vigiliis periculum augeatur. Prima luce sic ex castris proficiscuntur ut quibus esset persuasum non ab hoste sed ab homine amicissimo Ambiorige consilium datum, longissimo agmine maximisque impedimentis.

CHS. 32–37. *The Gauls ambushed the Roman column about two miles from the camp. The Romans resisted all day, and finally Sabinus entered into conference with Ambiorix, but was treacherously killed. Cotta died fighting, and, except for a few men who made their escape to Labienus, the Roman force was annihilated.*

XXXII

At hostes, postea quam ex nocturno fremitu vigiliisque de profectione eorum senserunt, collocatis insidiis bipertito in silvis opportuno atque occulto loco a milibus passuum circiter duobus Romanorum adventum exspectabant et, cum se maior pars agminis in magnam convallem demisisset, ex utraque parte eius vallis subito se ostenderunt, novissimosque premere et primos prohibere ascensu atque iniquissimo nostris loco proelium committere coeperunt.

XXXIII

Tum demum Titurius, qui nihil ante providisset, trepidare et concursare cohortisque disponere, haec tamen ipsa timide atque ut eum omnia deficere viderentur; quod plerumque eis accidere consuevit qui in ipso negotio consilium capere coguntur. At Cotta, qui cogitasset haec posse in itinere accidere atque ob eam causam profectionis auctor non fuisset, nulla in re communi saluti deerat et in appellandis cohortandisque militibus imperatoris et in pugna militis officia praestabat. Cum propter longitudinem agminis minus facile omnia per se obire et quid quoque loco faciendum esset providere possent, iusserunt pronuntiare ut impedimenta relinquerent atque in orbem consisterent. Quod consilium etsi in eiusmodi casu reprehendendum non est, tamen incommode accidit: nam et nostris militibus spem minuit et hostis ad pugnam alacriores effecit, quod non sine summo timore et desperatione id factum videbatur. Praeterea accidit, quod fieri necesse erat, ut vulgo milites ab signis discederent, quae quisque eorum carissima haberet ab impedimentis petere atque arripere properaret, clamore et fletu omnia complerentur.

XXXIV

At barbaris consilium non defuit. Nam duces eorum tota acie pronuntiare iusserunt, ne quis ab loco discederet, illorum esse praedam atque illis reservari quaecumque Romani reliquissent: proinde omnia in victoria posita existimarent. Erant et virtute et †numero pugnandi †pares. Nostri, tametsi ab duce et a fortuna deserebantur tamen omnem spem salutis in virtute ponebant, et quotiens quaeque cohors procurrerat, ab ea parte magnus numerus hostium cadebat. Qua re animadversa, Ambiorix pronuntiari iubet ut procul tela coiciant neu propius accedant et quam in partem Romani impetum fecerint cedant: levitate armorum et cotidiana exercitatione nihil his noceri posse: rursus se ad signa recipientis insequantur.

XXXV

Quo praecepto ab eis diligentissime observato, cum quaepiam cohors ex orbe excesserat atque impetum fecerat, hostes velocissime refugiebant. Interim eam partem nudari necesse erat et ab latere aperto tela recipi. Rursus cum in eum locum unde erant egressi reverti coeperant, et ab eis qui cesserant et ab eis qui proximi steterant circumveniebantur. Sin autem locum tenere vellent, nec virtuti locus relinquebatur neque ab tanta multitudine coiecta tela conferti vitare poterant. Tamen tot incommodis conflictati, multis vulneribus acceptis resistebant et magna parte diei consumpta, cum a prima luce ad horam octavam pugnaretur, nihil quod ipsis esset indignum committebant. Tum T. Balventio, qui superiore anno primum pilum duxerat, viro forti et magnae auctoritatis, utrumque femur tragula traicitur; Q. Lucanius eiusdem ordinis, fortissime pugnans, dum circumvento filio subvenit, interficitur; L. Cotta legatus omnis cohortis ordinesque adhortans in adversum os funda vulneratur.

XXXVI

His rebus permotus Q. Titurius, cum procul Ambiorigem suos cohortantem conspexisset, interpretem suum Cn. Pompeium ad eum mittit rogatum ut sibi militibusque parcat. Ille appellatus respondit: si velit secum colloqui, licere; sperare a multitudine impetrari posse, quod ad militum salutem pertineat;

ipsi vero nihil nocitum iri, inque eam rem se suam fidem interponere. Ille cum Cotta saucio communicat, si videatur, pugna ut excedant et cum Ambiorige una colloquantur: sperare ab eo de sua ac militum salute impetrari posse. Cotta se ad armatum hostem iturum negat atque in eo perseverat.

XXXVII

Sabinus quos in praesentia tribunos militum circum se habebat et primorum ordinum centuriones se sequi iubet et, cum propius Ambiorigem accessisset, iussus arma abicere imperatum facit suisque ut idem faciant imperat. Interim, dum de condicionibus inter se agunt longiorque consulto ab Ambiorige instituitur sermo, paulatim circumventus interficitur. Tum vero suo more victoriam conclamant atque ululatum tollunt impetuque in nostros facto ordines perturbant. Ibi L. Cotta pugnans interficitur cum maxima parte militum. Reliqui se in castra recipiunt unde erant egressi. Ex quibus L. Petrosidius aquilifer, cum magna multitudine hostium premeretur, aquilam intra vallum proiecit; ipse pro castris fortissime pugnans occiditur. Illi aegre ad noctem oppugnationem sustinent: noctu ad unum omnes desperata salute se ipsi interficiunt. Pauci ex proelio elapsi incertis itineribus per silvas ad T. Labienum legatum in hiberna perveniunt atque eum de rebus gestis certiorem faciunt.

(II) THE ATTACK ON CICERO

CHS. 38–41. *The next victim was Q. Cicero, who had not yet heard of the death of Sabinus and Cotta. Ambiorix persuaded the Aduatuci and the Nervii to attack Cicero's winter quarters. Cicero put up a vigorous defence and, at a conference, suggested to the Gauls that envoys be sent to Caesar.*

XXXVIII

Hac victoria sublatus Ambiorix statim cum equitatu in Aduatucos, qui erant eius regno finitimi, proficiscitur; neque noctem neque diem intermittit peditatumque sese subsequi iubet. Re demonstrata Aduatucisque concitatis, postero die in Nervios pervenit hortaturque ne sui in perpetuum liberandi atque ulciscendi Romanos pro eis quas acceperint iniuriis occasionem dimittant; interfectos esse legatos duo magnamque partem exercitus interisse demonstrat; nihil esse negoti subito oppressam legionem quae cum Cicerone hiemet interfici; se ad eam rem profitetur adiutorem. Facile hac oratione Nerviis persuadet.

XXXIX

Itaque confestim dimissis nuntiis ad Ceutrones, Grudios, Levacos, Pleumoxois, Geidumnos, qui omnes sub eorum imperio sunt, quam maximas manus possunt cogunt et de improviso ad Ciceronis hiberna advolant, nondum ad eum fama de Tituri morte perlata. Huic quoque accidit, quod fuit necesse, ut non nulli milites qui lignationis munitionisque causa in silvas discessissent repentino equitum adventu interciperentur. Eis circumventis, magna manu Eburones, Nervii, Aduatuci atque horum omnium socii et clientes legionem oppugnare incipiunt. Nostri celeriter ad arma concurrunt, vallum conscendunt. Aegre is dies sustentatur, quod omnem spem hostes in celeritate ponebant atque hanc adepti victoriam in perpetuum se fore victores confidebant.

XL

Mittuntur ad Caesarem confestim ab Cicerone litterae, magnis propositis praemiis, si pertulissent: obsessis omnibus viis missi intercipiuntur. Noctu ex materia quam munitionis causa comportaverant turres admodum centum xx excitantur incredibili celeritate; quae deesse operi videbantur perficiuntur. Hostes postero die multo maioribus coactis copiis castra oppugnant, fossam complent. Eadem ratione, qua pridie, ab nostris resistitur. Hoc idem reliquis deinceps fit diebus. Nulla pars nocturni temporis ad laborem intermittitur; non aegris, non vulneratis facultas quietis datur. Quaecumque ad proximi diei oppugnationem opus sunt noctu comparantur: multae praeustae sudes, magnus muralium pilorum numerus instituitur; turres contabulantur, pinnae loricaeque ex cratibus attexuntur. Ipse Cicero, cum tenuissima valetudine esset, ne nocturnum quidem sibi tempus ad quietem relinquebat, ut ultro militum concursu ac vocibus sibi parcere cogeretur.

XLI

Tunc duces principesque Nerviorum qui aliquem sermonis aditum causamque amicitiae cum Cicerone habebant colloqui sese velle dicunt. Facta potestate eadem quae Ambiorix cum Titurio egerat commemorant: omnem esse in armis Galliam; Germanos Rhenum transisse; Caesaris reliquorumque hiberna oppugnari. Addunt etiam de Sabini morte; Ambiorigem ostentant fidei faciendae causa. Errare eos dicunt, si quicquam ab eis praesidi sperent qui suis rebus diffidant; sese tamen hoc esse in Ciceronem populumque Romanum animo ut nihil nisi hiberna recusent atque hanc inveterascere consuetudinem nolint: licere illis incolumibus per se ex hibernis discedere et quascumque in partis velint sine metu proficisci. Cicero ad haec unum modo respondit: non esse consuetudinem populi Romani accipere ab hoste armato condicionem: si ab armis discedere velint, se adiutore utantur legatosque ad Caesarem mittant; sperare pro eius iustitia quae petierint impetraturos.

CHS. 42–43. *The Nervii, by way of reply, invested Cicero's camp with a rampart, ditch, and towers of the Roman type, and, after a week's siege, made a desperate assault. They were, however, driven off.*

XLII

Ab hac spe repulsi Nervii vallo pedum IX et fossa pedum XV hiberna cingunt. Haec et superiorum annorum consuetudine ab nobis cognoverant et quos clam de exercitu habebant captivos ab eis docebantur; sed nulla ferramentorum copia quae esset ad hunc usum idonea, gladiis caespites circumcidere, manibus sagulisque terram exhaurire videbantur. Qua quidem ex re hominum multitudo cognosci potuit: nam minus horis tribus milium [p̄. xv] in circuitu III munitionem perfecerunt; reliquisque diebus turris ad altitudinem valli, falces testudinesque, quas idem captivi docuerant, parare ac facere coeperunt.

XLIII

Septimo oppugnationis die maximo coorto vento ferventis fusili ex argilla glandis fundis et fervefacta iacula in casas, quae more Gallico stramentis erant tectae, iacere coeperunt. Hae celeriter ignem comprehenderunt et venti magnitudine in omnem locum castrorum distulerunt. Hostes maximo clamore, sicuti parta iam atque explorata victoria, turris testudinesque agere et scalis vallum ascendere coeperunt. At tanta militum virtus atque ea praesentia animi fuit ut, cum ubique flamma torrerentur maximaque telorum multitudine premerentur suaque omnia impedimenta atque omnis fortunas conflagrare intellegerent, non modo demigrandi causa de vallo decederet nemo sed paene ne respiceret quidem quisquam, ac tum omnes acerrime fortissimeque pugnarent. Hic dies nostris longe gravissimus fuit, sed tamen hunc habuit eventum ut eo die maximus numerus hostium vulneraretur atque interficeretur, ut se sub ipso vallo constipaverant recessumque primis ultimi non dabant. Paulum quidem intermissa flamma et quodam loco turri adacta et contingente vallum, tertiae cohortis centuriones ex eo quo stabant loco recesserunt suosque omnis removerunt; nutu vocibusque hostis, si introire vellent, vocare coeperunt: quorum progredi ausus est nemo. Tum ex omni parte lapidibus coiectis deturbati, turrisque succensa est.

CH. 44. *In passing, Caesar described an incident of the siege in which two centurions, T. Pullo and L. Vorenus, were involved.*

XLIV

Erant in ea legione fortissimi viri, centuriones, qui primis ordinibus appropinquarent, T. Pullo et L. Vorenus. Hi perpetuas inter se controversias habebant, quinam anteferretur, omnibusque annis de locis summis simultatibus contendebant. Ex his Pullo, cum acerrime ad munitiones pugnaretur, 'Quid dubitas,' inquit, 'Vorene? aut quem locum tuae pro laude virtutis spectas? hic dies de nostris controversiis iudicabit.' Haec cum dixisset, procedit extra munitiones, quaeque pars hostium confertissima est visa irrumpit. Ne Vorenus quidem sese vallo continet sed omnium veritus existimationem subsequitur. Tum mediocri spatio relicto Pullo pilum in hostis immittit, atque unum ex multitudine procurrentem traicit; quo percusso et exanimato, hunc scutis protegunt, in hostem tela universi coiciunt neque dant regrediendi facultatem. Transfigitur scutum Pulloni et verutum in balteo defigitur. Avertit hic casus vaginam et gladium educere conanti dextram moratur manum, impeditumque hostes circumsistunt. Succurrit inimicus illi Vorenus et laboranti subvenit. Ad hunc se confestim a Pullone omnis multitudo convertit; illum veruto arbitrantur occisum. Gladio comminus rem gerit Vorenus, atque uno interfecto reliquos paulum propellit: dum cupidius instat, in locum deiectus inferiorem concidit. Huic rursus circumvento fert subsidium Pullo, atque ambo incolumes compluribus interfectis summa cum laude sese intra munitiones recipiunt. Sic fortuna in contentione et certamine utrumque versavit, ut alter alteri inimicus auxilio salutique esset neque diiudicari posset, uter utri virtute anteferendus videretur.

CHS. 45–48. *After many others had failed, a Nervian slave succeeded in conveying a message to Caesar at Samarobriva, who immediately made plans for relieving Cicero. (i) He started out himself at the head of the legion which was stationed at Samarobriva and was joined by Fabius' legion (from among the Morini) on the way. (ii) He summoned M. Crassus, who was stationed among the Bellovaci, to take his place at Samarobriva. (iii) He asked Labienus to advance from the territory of the Treveri and make a diversion from the south-east. Owing to his own precarious position, however, Labienus was unable to move.*

XLV

Quanto erat in dies gravior atque asperior oppugnatio, et maxime quod magna parte militum confecta vulneribus res ad paucitatem defensorum pervenerat, tanto crebriores litterae nuntiique ad Caesarem mittebantur; quorum pars deprehensa in conspectu nostrorum militum cum cruciatu necabatur. Erat unus intus Nervius, nomine Vertico, loco natus honesto, qui a prima obsidione ad Ciceronem perfugerat, suamque ei fidem praestiterat. Hic servo spe libertatis magnisque persuadet praemiis ut litteras ad Caesarem deferat. Has ille in iaculo inligatas effert, et Gallus inter Gallos sine ulla suspicione versatus ad Caesarem pervenit. Ab eo de periculis Ciceronis legionisque cognoscitur.

XLVI

Caesar, acceptis litteris hora circiter undecima diei, statim nuntium in Bellovacos ad M. Crassum quaestorem mittit, cuius hiberna aberant ab eo milia passuum XXV; iubet media nocte legionem proficisci celeriterque ad se venire. Exit cum nuntio Crassus. Alterum ad C. Fabium legatum mittit, ut in Atrebatum finis legionem adducat, qua sibi iter faciendum sciebat. Scribit Labieno, si rei publicae commodo facere posset, cum legione ad finis Nerviorum veniat. Reliquam partem exercitus, quod paulo aberat longius, non putat exspectandam; equites circiter quadringentos ex proximis hibernis colligit.

XLVII

Hora circiter tertia ab antecursoribus de Crassi adventu certior factus, eo die milia passuum xx procedit. Crassum Samarobrivae praeficit legionemque attribuit, quod ibi impedimenta exercitus, obsides civitatum, litteras publicas, frumentumque omne quod eo tolerandae hiemis causa devexerat relinquebat. Fabius, ut imperatum erat, non ita multum moratus in itinere cum legione occurrit. Labienus, interitu Sabini et caede cohortium cognita, cum omnes ad eum Treverorum copiae venissent veritus ne, si ex hibernis fugae similem profectionem fecisset, hostium impetum sustinere non posset, praesertim quos recenti victoria efferri sciret, litteras Caesari remittit: quanto cum periculo legionem ex hibernis educturus esset; rem gestam in Eburonibus perscribit; docet omnis equitatus peditatusque copias Treverorum tria milia passuum longe ab suis castris consedisse.

XLVIII

Caesar, consilio eius probato, etsi opinione trium legionum deiectus ad duas redierat, tamen unum communis salutis auxilium in celeritate ponebat. Venit magnis itineribus in Nerviorum finis. Ibi ex captivis cognoscit quae apud Ciceronem gerantur quantoque in periculo res sit. Tum cuidam ex equitibus Gallis magnis praemiis persuadet uti ad Ciceronem epistolam deferat. Hanc Graecis conscriptam litteris mittit, ne intercepta epistola nostra ab hostibus consilia cognoscantur. Si adire non possit monet ut tragulam cum epistola ad ammentum deligata intra munitionem castrorum abiciat. In litteris scribit se cum legionibus profectum celeriter adfore; hortatur ut pristinam virtutem retineat. Gallus periculum veritus, ut erat praeceptum, tragulam mittit. Haec casu ad turrim adhaesit neque ab nostris biduo animadversa tertio die a quodam milite conspicitur, dempta ad Ciceronem defertur. Ille perlectam in conventu militum recitat, maximaque omnis laetitia adficit. Tum fumi incendiorum procul videbantur, quae res omnem dubitationem adventus legionum expulit.

CHS. 49–52. *The advance of Caesar caused the Gauls to abandon the siege of Cicero's camp. They were enticed to attack on unfavourable ground and were utterly defeated. Caesar was then able to join Cicero.*

XLIX

Galli re cognita per exploratores obsidionem relinquunt, ad Caesarem omnibus copiis contendunt. Haec erant armatae circiter milia LX. Cicero data facultate Gallum ab eodem Verticone, quem supra demonstravimus, repetit qui litteras ad Caesarem deferat. Hunc admonet iter caute diligenterque faciat. Perscribit in litteris hostis ab se discessisse omnemque ad eum multitudinem convertisse. Quibus litteris circiter media nocte Caesar allatis suos facit certiores eosque ad dimicandum animo confirmat. Postera die luce prima movet castra et circiter milia passuum quattuor progressus trans vallem et rivum multitudinem hostium conspicatur. Erat magni periculi res tantulis copiis iniquo loco dimicare; tum, quoniam obsidione liberatum Ciceronem sciebat, aequo animo remittendum de celeritate existimabat. Consedit et quam aequissimo loco potest castra communit, atque haec, etsi erant exigua per se, vix hominum milium septem, praesertim nullis cum impedimentis, tamen angustiis viarum quam maxime potest contrahit eo consilio ut in summam contemptionem hostibus veniat. Interim speculatoribus in omnis partis dimissis explorat quo commodissime itinere valles transiri possit.

L

Eo die parvulis equestribus proeliis ad aquam factis, utrique sese suo loco continent: Galli, quod ampliores copias, quae nondum convenerant, exspectabant; Caesar, si forte timoris simulatione hostis in suum locum elicere posset, ut citra vallem pro castris proelio contenderet; si id efficere non posset, ut exploratis itineribus minore cum periculo vallem rivumque transiret. Prima luce hostium equitatus ad castra accedit proeliumque cum nostris equitibus committit. Caesar consulto equites cedere seque in castra recipere iubet; simul ex omnibus partibus castra altiore vallo muniri portasque obstrui atque in his administrandis rebus quam maxime concursari et cum simulatione agi timoris iubet.

LI

Quibus omnibus rebus hostes invitati copias traducunt aciemque iniquo loco constituunt, nostris vero etiam de vallo deductis propius accedunt et tela intra munitionem ex omnibus partibus coiciunt, praeconibusque circummissis pronuntiari iubent, seu quis Gallus seu Romanus velit ante horam tertiam ad se transire, sine periculo licere: post id tempus non fore potestatem; ac sic nostros contempserunt, ut obstructis in speciem portis singulis ordinibus caespitum, quod ea non posse introrumpere videbantur, alii vallum manu scindere, alii fossas complere inciperent. Tum Caesar omnibus portis eruptione facta equitatuque emisso celeriter hostis in fugam dat, sic uti omnino pugnandi causa resisteret nemo, magnumque ex eis numerum occidit atque omnis armis exuit.

LII

Longius prosequi veritus, quod silvae paludesque intercedebant neque etiam parvulo detrimento illorum locum relinqui videbat, omnibus suis incolumibus copiis eodem die ad Ciceronem pervenit. Institutas turris, testudines, munitionesque hostium admiratur. Legione producta, cognoscit non decimum quemque esse reliquum militem sine vulnere. Ex eis omnibus iudicat rebus quanto cum periculo et quanta cum virtute res sint administratae. Ciceronem pro eius merito legionemque collaudat; centuriones singillatim tribunosque militum appellat, quorum egregiam fuisse virtutem testimonio Ciceronis cognoverat. De casu Sabini et Cottae certius ex captivis cognoscit. Postero die contione habita rem gestam proponit; milites consolatur et confirmat: quod detrimentum culpa et temeritate legati sit acceptum, hoc aequiore animo ferendum docet, quod beneficio deorum immortalium et virtute eorum expiato incommodo neque hostibus diutina laetatio neque ipsis longior dolor relinquatur.

CHS. 53–54. *Caesar sent Fabius back to his winter quarters among the Morini, but decided himself to stay with three legions in the neighbourhood of Samarobriva for the whole winter. Reports of Gallic intrigues were constantly arriving. The worst news concerned the tribes of the coast of Normandy, who plotted to attack L. Roscius, but changed their minds when they heard of Caesar's victory, and the Senones, who expelled a client king whom Caesar had set over them and defied Caesar himself.*

LIII

Interim ad Labienum per Remos incredibili celeritate de victoria Caesaris fama perfertur, ut, cum ab hibernis Ciceronis milia passuum abesset circiter LX eoque post horam nonam diei Caesar pervenisset, ante mediam noctem ad portas castrorum clamor oreretur, quo clamore significatio victoriae gratulatioque ab Remis Labieno fieret. Hac fama ad Treveros perlata, Indutiomarus, qui postero die castra Labieni oppugnare decreverat, noctu profugit copiasque omnis in Treveros reducit. Caesar Fabium cum sua legione remittit in hiberna, ipse cum tribus legionibus circum Samarobrivam trinis hibernis hiemare constituit et, quod tanti motus Galliae exstiterant, totam hiemem ipse ad exercitum manere decrevit. Nam illo incommodo de Sabini morte perlato omnes fere Galliae civitates de bello consultabant, nuntios legationesque in omnis partis dimittebant et quid reliqui consili caperent atque unde initium belli fieret explorabant, nocturnaque in locis desertis concilia habebant. Neque ullum fere totius hiemis tempus sine sollicitudine Caesaris intercessit, quin aliquem de consiliis ac motu Gallorum nuntium acciperet. In his ab L. Roscio [quaestore], quem legioni tertiae decimae praefecerat, certior factus est magnas Gallorum copias earum civitatum quae Aremoricae appellantur oppugnandi sui causa convenisse neque longius milia passuum octo ab hibernis suis afuisse, sed nuntio allato de victoria Caesaris discessisse, adeo ut fugae similis discessus videretur.

LIV

At Caesar, principibus cuiusque civitatis ad se evocatis, alias territando, cum se scire quae fierent denuntiaret, alias cohortando magnam partem Galliae in officio tenuit. Tamen Senones, quae est civitas in primis firma et magnae inter Gallos auctoritatis, Cavarinum, quem Caesar apud eos regem constituerat, cuius frater Moritasgus adventu in Galliam Caesaris cuiusque maiores regnum obtinuerant, interficere publico consilio conati, cum ille praesensisset ac profugisset, usque ad finis insecuti regno domoque expulerunt et, missis ad Caesarem satisfaciendi causa legatis, cum is omnem ad se senatum venire iussisset, dicto audientes non fuerunt. Tantum apud homines barbaros valuit esse aliquos repertos principes inferendi belli tantamque omnibus voluntatum commutationem attulit, ut praeter Aeduos et Remos, quos praecipuo semper honore Caesar habuit, alteros pro vetere ac perpetua erga populum Romanum fide, alteros pro recentibus Gallici belli officiis, nulla fere civitas fuerit non suspecta nobis. Idque adeo haud scio mirandumne sit, cum compluribus aliis de causis, tum maxime quod ei qui virtute belli omnibus gentibus praeferebantur tantum se eius opinionis deperdidisse ut a populo Romano imperia perferrent gravissime dolebant.

(III) The Attack on Labienus

Chs. 55–58. *The Treveri, instigated by Indutiomarus, attacked the camp of Labienus, which was, however, well situated for defence. Labienus succeeded in collecting cavalry from the neighbouring tribes, and, by feigning fear, put Indutiomarus off his guard. In a sudden sortie, Labienus' cavalry defeated the Gallic troops and killed Indutiomarus. The restiveness in Gaul then abated.*

LV

Treveri vero atque Indutiomarus totius hiemis nullum tempus intermiserunt quin trans Rhenum legatos mitterent, civitates sollicitarent, pecunias pollicerentur, magna parte exercitus nostri interfecta multo minorem superesse dicerent partem. Neque tamen ulli civitati Germanorum persuaderi potuit ut Rhenum transiret, cum se bis expertos dicerent, Ariovisti bello et Tencterorum transitu: non esse amplius fortunam temptaturos. Hac spe lapsus Indutiomarus nihilo minus copias cogere, exercere, a finitimis equos parare, exsules damnatosque tota Gallia magnis praemiis ad se allicere coepit. Ac tantam sibi iam his rebus in Gallia auctoritatem comparaverat ut undique ad eum legationes concurrerent, gratiam atque amicitiam publice privatimque peterent.

LVI

Ubi intellexit ultro ad se veniri, altera ex parte Senones Carnutesque conscientia facinoris instigari, altera Nervios Aduatucosque bellum Romanis parare, neque sibi voluntariorum copias defore si ex finibus suis progredi coepisset, armatum concilium indicit. Hoc more Gallorum est initium belli, quo lege communi omnes puberes armati convenire consuerunt: qui ex eis novissimus convenit, in conspectu multitudinis omnibus cruciatibus adfectus necatur. In eo concilio Cingetorigem, alterius principem factionis, generum suum, quem supra demonstravimus Caesaris secutum fidem ab eo non discessisse, hostem iudicat bonaque eius publicat. His rebus confectis, in concilio pronuntiat arcessitum se a Senonibus et Carnutibus aliisque compluribus Galliae civitatibus; huc iturum per finis Remorum eorumque agros populaturum ac prius quam id faciat castra Labieni oppugnaturum. Quae fieri velit praecipit.

LVII

Labienus, cum et loci natura et manu munitissimis castris sese teneret, de suo ac legionis periculo nihil timebat; ne quam occasionem rei bene gerendae dimitteret cogitabat. Itaque a Cingetorige atque eius propinquis oratione Indutiomari cognita quam in concilio habuerat, nuntios mittit ad finitimas civitates equitesque undique evocat; his certum diem conveniendi dicit. Interim prope cotidie cum omni equitatu Indutiomarus sub castris eius vagabatur, alias ut situm castrorum cognosceret, alias colloquendi aut territandi causa; equites plerumque omnes tela intra vallum coiciebant. Labienus suos intra munitionem continebat timorisque opinionem quibuscumque poterat rebus augebat.

LVIII

Cum maiore in dies contemptione Indutiomarus ad castra accederet, nocte una intromissis equitibus omnium finitimarum civitatum quos accersendos curaverat, tanta diligentia omnis suos custodiis intra castra continuit, ut nulla ratione ea res enuntiari aut ad Treveros perferri posset. Interim ex consuetudine cotidiana Indutiomarus ad castra accedit atque ibi magnam partem diei consumit; equites tela coiciunt et magna cum contumelia verborum nostros ad pugnam evocant. Nullo ab nostris data responso, ubi visum est, sub vesperum dispersi ac dissipati discedunt. Subito Labienus duabus portis omnem equitatum emittit; praecipit atque interdicit, proterritis hostibus atque in fugam coiectis (quod fore, sicut accidit, videbat) unum omnes peterent Indutiomarum, neu quis quem prius vulneret quam illum interfectum viderit, quod mora reliquorum spatium nactum illum effugere nolebat; magna proponit eis qui occiderint praemia; summittit cohortis equitibus subsidio. Comprobat hominis consilium fortuna et, cum unum omnes peterent, in ipso fluminis vado deprehensus Indutiomarus interficitur, caputque eius refertur in castra; redeuntes equites quos possunt consectantur atque occidunt. Hac re cognita, omnes Eburonum et Nerviorum quae convenerant copiae discedunt, pauloque habuit post id factum Caesar quietiorem Galliam.

NOTES

Caesar's first expedition to Britain, which he had undertaken in August, 55 B.C. in order to reconnoitre the south-east parts of the island, had appeared to end on a note of success. Immediately on landing Caesar defeated the Britons in an engagement and forced them to sue for peace, and although a storm that arose in the Channel damaged the ships in which he had crossed and encouraged the Britons to renew hostilities and to attack his camp in force, they were again defeated and once more sued for peace. Thus Caesar was able to represent his expedition as successful, and a thanksgiving of twenty days was voted in Rome. But what, in fact, had he achieved ? Of the questions on which he sought information, concerning the size of the island, the number and strength of the tribes, their mode of fighting and institutions, and the existence of suitable harbours (Book IV, ch. xx), he can have got the answer to very few. One lesson he certainly learnt and turned to good advantage, viz. that the draught of his ships was too big to make the landing of troops easy on a shelving coast, and for this reason he had his ships made shallower for the great invasion of the following summer (Book V, ch. I). He learnt other things too, *e.g.* that the British chariot-attack was not dangerous to a legion in battle-formation, the chief advantage of chariots being that, if the Romans lacked cavalry, they rendered the enemy difficult to pursue after a defeat, or again, that it was not an easy matter, in the absence of a good harbour, to keep a fleet safely on the British coast. But he does not seem always to have put his information to much practical purpose. Thus, in 54 B.C., he brought only 2000 cavalry, which in the event proved an inadequate number (Book V, ch. VIII), and his reliance on the devastating effect of a swift initial defeat led him to ignore the warning of the storms of the previous years. He attacked the Britons immediately on landing without taking measures to protect his ships and, in consequence, had them severely damaged in a gale (Book V, ch. IX).

I

1. **L. Domitio App. Claudio consulibus,** *i.e.* the year 54 B.C.

2. **ab hibernis Caesar in Italiam.** The new consuls entered on their term of office on Jan. 1, 54 B.C., and even if we allow for the fact that the official calendar was out of joint and was about a month in advance of the real time, Caesar seems to have spent an unusually long time in his winter quarters, since he had returned from Britain the previous September. We may guess that he was occupied with two matters especially: (i) his plans for the second invasion of Britain, which were elaborate. As two tribes only in Britain had sent their promised hostages, he realised that the conquest of the island was not going to be easy; (ii) unrest in Gaul, which threatened his whole scheme of conquering Britain and ultimately proved its undoing.

Caesar's province really consisted of three provinces, united temporarily under one command, viz. Illyricum, Gallia Cisalpina, and Gallia Transalpina (Introduction, p. 10). In the peaceful portions of this vast area, Caesar's duties were of a civil nature—arranging finances and taxation, and holding courts of law in the *conventus* or 'circuits' into which the province was divided. It was his custom to spend the winter attending to this business.

3. **legatis . . . quos legionibus praefecerat.** See Introduction, p. 24.

4. **navis aedificandas.** The Roman navy consisted of warships (*naves longae*), transports (*naves onerariae*), and various types of light craft. The standard warship in the third century B.C. had been the quinquireme, and though it is not known for certain what this type of vessel was like or how it was propelled, the most likely suggestion is that 'it was a comparatively light galley of shallow draught and low free-board, probably propelled by a single row of long oars with five men to each' (*Companion to Latin Studies*, p. 494).

Triremes also were used and in later centuries the proportion of them seems to have increased. In the first century B.C., two new types of vessel came into use, viz. the bireme (Pl. VIII, *a*) and the 'Liburnian.' The latter was modelled originally on a swift Illyrian boat with a ram, but by the Romans it was often given the form of a bireme: it was used both for scouting and for fighting.

7. **subductiones.** The plural implies frequent acts. The verb is *subducere* ('haul up' or 'beach') and the opposite process is represented by *deducere* ('launch').

In the first invasion Caesar had hauled up his warships on to the beach, but had left his transports riding at anchor nearby (Book IV, ch. XXIX). Knowing the effect of a swift initial defeat on the Celtic temperament, he was anxious to come to grips at once. A sudden storm sprang up, however, and damaged both warships and transports alike, seriously jeopardising the whole expedition. For the second invasion he had the ships made shallower so that they could be dragged more easily out of harm's way.

8. **nostro mari,** *i.e.* the Mediterranean.

10. **minus magnos.** The comparative smallness of the waves in the Channel seems to be due, not so much to the swiftly changing tides, as to the shallowness and narrowness of the waters.

13. **actuarias imperat fieri,** *i.e.* to be built for rowing as well as sailing. Caesar, Cicero, and post-Augustan writers use *imperare* with the accusative and infinitive construction only when the infinitive is passive or deponent.

15. **ex Hispania.** The esparto grass of Spain was used for making ropes and rigging. Iron for anchors and copper for use in bronze fittings might be had from either Gaul or Spain.

16. **conventibus,** 'assizes.'

17. **a Pirustis.** This tribe lived on the southern border of the province of Illyricum.

26. **sese . . . persecuturum.** You will find that Caesar hardly ever uses *esse* in the future infinitive.

Notice the twofold manner of dealing with this minor

frontier incident: (i) Caesar appoints arbitrators to assess the amount of the reparation to be made; (ii) he exacts hostages as a guarantee of good behaviour for the future.

II

2. **ad exercitum,** the army which he left stationed for the winter of 55–54 B.C. among the Belgae.

5. **eius generis cuius . . . possint.** There are three examples of loose writing in these lines: (i) *cuius,* where we should have expected *quod,* is due to the attraction of *generis*; (ii) in the phrase *neque multum abesse ab eo quin,* the *ab eo* would normally be followed by *ut,* not *quin*: on the other hand, *non multum abesse quin* is a common phrase, and the two are confused; (iii) *paucis diebus* seems unnecessary after *neque multum* ('almost ready for launching in a few days').

10. **ad portum Itium.** See note on ch. v, line 1. In describing the first invasion, Caesar had not mentioned his port of embarkation by name.

15. **expeditis,** 'lightly equipped.' The word is used by Caesar with at least two meanings: (i) as here, 'in light marching order,' *i.e.* without heavy baggage, but presumably with packs and entrenching tools; (ii) 'stripped for action,' *i.e.* carrying nothing that was not immediately required for fighting.

Treverorum. See Index of Proper Names. This tribe had sent cavalry to Caesar against the Belgae in 57 B.C., but had deserted when they thought the campaign was going against him. They were now planning revolt again, and it was clearly unsafe to leave them as a centre of disaffection in his rear. On the other hand, Caesar did not wish to spend much time dealing with them now, as his preparations for invading Britain were well advanced. It is clear in ch. IV that he did little more than temporarily patch up the trouble.

16. **concilia,** meetings of the Gallic chiefs which Caesar turned to his own account. He called them in the spring of each year to test their loyalty and fix the number of

cavalrymen each should provide. In these *concilia* lay the germ of the provincial assembly which was later to meet at Lyons.

17. **Transrhenanos.** This qualification is added because Caesar elsewhere classes as Germans various tribes of Belgium.

III

3. **supra,** *i.e.* in Books II and III of the Commentaries.

10. **cogere,** to be taken, like *parare,* with *instituit.*

12. **Arduennam.** See Index of Proper Names.

18. **privatim.** The position of the adverb gives it the force of an adjective agreeing with *rebus.*

IV

7. **consolatus.** Indutiomarus needed reassuring that his relatives would be well treated.

11. **cum . . . tum. . . .** Correlatives: see Vocabulary.

merito eius, literally 'in accordance with his (Cingetorix') merit.' Caesar knew that Cingetorix deserved well of him.

Notice how Caesar astutely exploits the rivalry of Indutiomarus and Cingetorix for his own purposes. He does not try to reconcile them, but by increasing the power of Cingetorix, he makes him both grateful for the kindness and capable of repaying it, should occasion arise.

V

1. **ad portum Itium.** In describing the first expedition Caesar had not mentioned the name of his port of departure. The exact identity of Portus Itius has been disputed, and arguments have been advanced in favour of both Boulogne and Wissant. Writers of the first century A.D. speak of Boulogne (Gesoriacum) as the most famous harbour on the north coast of Gaul and the regular port of departure for Britain, and various other considerations suggest that the site of Portus Itius is to be sought here rather than at Wissant. Portus Itius may be an adaptation of the pre-Roman name of Boulogne, which was called Gesoriacum

after the time of Claudius and Bononia after the third century A.D.

Rice Holmes' calculations of the dates of Caesar's journey are illuminating. 'Caesar left Blandeno in Cisalpine Gaul about the 30th of April (of the Julian Calendar) and, after the movements described in chs. II–IV, arrived at Portus Itius about the 11th of June. He had therefore posted across Gaul at the rate of 50 miles a day or more; and there is no more conclusive proof of the hold which he had already obtained upon the Gallic tribes than the fact that he was able to count, as securely as in Italy, upon finding horses ready for each successive stage' (*Caesar, De Bello Gallico*, p. 174). Caesar was accompanied on this journey by Q. Cicero, younger brother of the famous orator, serving as *legatus*.

2. **cum legionibus.** Besides the legionaries, the Roman army contained certain auxiliary forces (*e.g.* cavalry and light troops), recruited from the provincials. Elsewhere in his account of the Gallic Wars, Caesar mentions that he had Numidian and Spanish cavalry, Cretan archers, and Balearic slingers under his command, and it is known that he recruited cavalry in Gaul. In the first invasion of Britain, cavalry, slingers, and archers took part (Book IV, ch. XXV), though, as it turned out, the cavalry were unable to cross the Channel.

3. **Meldis.** See Index of Proper Names. Notice the distance which these ships had to travel down the Marne and the Seine (Map, p. 13).

The force encamped at Boulogne consisted of 8 legions (about 35,000 men) together with slingers and archers and 4000 Gallic cavalry. The fleet numbered more than 800 vessels of various kinds, including 28 warships, 540 transports, and about 200 ships provided by private owners such as merchants and adventurers who wished to follow the fortune of the expedition. Of this force Caesar left behind with Labienus 3 legions and 2000 cavalry to watch his base and commissariat. He had in addition the 60 ships mentioned in this chapter, which were weather-bound at the mouth of the Seine.

7. **equitatus totius Galliae,** not the cavalry which the

whole of Gaul *could* provide, but that which was levied by Caesar. In the revolt of 52 B.C., the Gauls themselves collected 8000 cavalry against Caesar.

VI

1. **Dumnorix Aeduus.** See Index of Proper Names. Coins bearing the legend DUBNOREX testify to the authority which this chief exercised (Pl. II, *b*, iv).

2. **antea,** *i.e.* in Book I of the Commentaries.

3. **cupidum rerum novarum . . . auctoritatis.** Note the change of construction. *Imperi* is objective genitive after *cupidum*: *magni animi* and *magnae auctoritatis* are 'genitives of quality or description,' not, of course, to be taken with *cupidum.*

7. **regnum civitatis deferri.** Roman generals sometimes appointed client kings to rule over conquered tribes, partly to reward loyalty, partly to enable them to fix responsibility for the maintenance of order. The employment of 'client kings' later became common in difficult parts of the Roman Empire and on frontiers. Caesar used these appointments with great astuteness (see note on ch. IV, line 11), but the practice raised many false hopes and his appointments led to discontent amongst unsuccessful aspirants (see ch. XXV). Notice the use of the present infinitive. Dumnorix does not say that Caesar had made the offer, but that it was 'on its way.'

8. **neque,** equivalent to *neque tamen* ('but . . . not . . .').

10. **hospitibus.** It was a custom amongst prominent Romans to make agreements with individual foreigners whereby, in return for help and patronage and, in some cases, the grant of Roman citizenship, the latter furnished hospitality to the former. This tie was known as *hospitium* and those united by it as *hospites.* The practice had great practical use in a country ill-provided with inns.

12. **partim quod . . . timeret, partim quod . . . diceret.** *timeret* is in the subjunctive because it expresses what Dumnorix said, and the second verb would more correctly have been *impediretur,* without *diceret,* since the subjunctive

alone would have implied that the reason was only alleged; or the sentence might have run *partim quia . . . sese dicebat impediri*, since his saying it was an actual fact. What Caesar has written is confused, though it is a confusion into which several Latin writers fell.

16. The infinitives from here to the end of the chapter are difficult and the text is not above suspicion. As they stand, *sollicitare*, *sevocare*, and *hortari* depend on *coepit*; *territare*, *interponere*, and *poscere* are historic infinitives and must be translated as main verbs; *fieri* and *esse* (in *id esse consilium*) are in the accusative and infinitive construction, after the idea of 'saying' contained in *metu territare*.

22. **fidem reliquis interponere** seems to mean 'gave them his pledged word,' since Caesar uses *fidem suam interponere* in this sense elsewhere.

VII

4. **longius.** The comparative in Latin may be translated in various ways. Thus *longius* may mean 'further,' 'too far,' 'rather far,' and 'at all far,' etc. Here it seems to mean 'too far.'

7. **commoratus,** not 'having delayed' merely, nor yet equivalent to a present participle, but used, as the past participle is often used, to express cause.

It has been suggested that Caesar was detained, not by the weather, but for political reasons—rumours from Rome or the uneasy state of Gaul.

14. **cum equitibus Aeduorum.** Dumnorix was in command of the Aeduan contingent of cavalry, as he had been in 58 B.C. when he first served under Caesar.

19. **nihil hunc . . . pro sano facturum,** 'would not behave at all like a rational being'; *sano* is masculine.

21. **enim,** '(and he was right in thinking so) for.'

25. **hominem,** 'the fellow': the word shows ill-feeling. Caesar takes the responsibility for this summary execution (*ut erat imperatum*). For the moment he achieved his object and the Gallic nobles were terrified into silence, but secret

resentment remained and found expression in the great rebellion of 52 B.C.

VIII

1. **Labieno.** See Index of Proper Names. The fact that Caesar left his ablest officer and over a third of the total troops assembled at Portus Itius to guard his bases, watch his supplies, and keep an eye on Gaul, shows the importance of the task.

3. **portus.** Just as in the previous year Caesar had used two harbours, so in 54 B.C. he thought it advisable to have more than one port under his control: hence the plural.

5. **pro tempore et pro re,** *i.e.* as occasion and circumstances should demand.

6. **pari . . . quem . . .,** equivalent to *pari . . . atque. . . .*

7. **ad solis occasum.** The date cannot be calculated exactly, but it was probably about July 6. Caesar embarked on the ebb; the tide turned about 10 p.m. and carried him up-Channel. About midnight the wind failed, and the tide carried him too far east, so that when, between 3 and 4 a.m., it became light enough to see the coast (the South Foreland), it was receding behind him on the port side. The tide turned down-Channel about 4 a.m., and taking advantage of the slack water that preceded it, Caesar ordered his men to get out their oars.

13. **egressum.** The point at which Caesar landed in Britain, like his port of departure from Gaul, has caused much discussion, and a dozen different places have been proposed. From his account of the first invasion, we gather that on reaching the British coast, Caesar found steep cliffs, occupied by the natives with an armed force; so he sailed on for seven miles until he came to a place where the beach was flat and open. The most likely theory is that Caesar reached the British coast at Dover and, finding the cliffs occupied, rode at anchor off Dover until the tide turned up-Channel and a breeze from the south sprang up, which enabled him to bring his fleet round the South Foreland and run it aground after passing the

point where the cliffs end (Kingsdown). On this view, his landing-place would be somewhere near Walmer or Deal, where the shelving beach may well be described as 'flat and open.' He can hardly have sailed farther north than Deal or he would have found the sheltered harbour that at that time lay inland from Pegwell Bay between the Isle of Thanet and the mainland (Pl. IX). Caesar's failure to discover this harbour has been called 'the blunder that marred the entire expedition.' It was protected from storms by the Isle of Thanet and was precisely the kind of harbour that, at the beginning of the first invasion, he said he was seeking. The armies of the Emperor Claudius later used it as their base for the conquest of Britain, and, on what was at that time a small island overlooking the harbour, the Roman fort Rutupiae (Richborough) was built, of which extensive remains have been excavated.

In the present passage, Caesar does not make it clear whether his landing-place in the second expedition was the same as the previous year or another which he had chosen then. It must, however, have been roughly in the same place, viz. north of Kingsdown where the cliffs end and the flat shore begins, and far enough south of Sandwich for him not to notice the harbour.

22. **quas sui quisque commodi fecerat.** *sui commodi* is best explained as a genitive of purpose ('for his own convenience'). It is difficult to explain this usage in simple language, but if we start by saying that the function of the genitive case is to define a noun, then we may say that the noun defined in this sentence is the action implied in *quas fecerat* and that it is defined by being expressed as belonging to a purpose.

24. **in superiora loca,** viz. the high ground just west of Canterbury, overlooking the Great Stour, whose passage the Britons meant to deny to the Romans. The hill-fort of Bigbury is situated here.

IX

3. **cohortibus decem.** These were numerically equal to a legion, but the form of expression shows that the cohorts were selected from the 5 legions.

5. **contendit . . . praefecit.** *praefecit* is parallel with *contendit* and is not to be taken as another reason for his having no fears for his fleet. The datives in this sentence and the triple repetition of *navibus* are a little ungainly. *praesidio* in line 4 is predicative; *navibus* in each case expresses the indirect object, though that in line 7 would more normally be a genitive, since *praefecit* already has one indirect object in *praesidio*. Tr. 'the guard over the ships.'

6. **in litore molli atque aperto.** *aperto* means that the approach was free from rocks, while *molli* implies gently sloping and having a soft surface. Reading between the lines, one can see that Caesar is here excusing himself for the disaster which later occurred to the ships (ch. x). Knowing the effect that an early defeat would have on the Britons, he was anxious to force an engagement as soon as possible and for that reason was loathe to spend valuable time hauling up his ships on shore. After his experience the year before, it is almost unbelievable that he would take such a risk.

10. **ad flumen,** the Great Stour.

13. **locum . . . egregie et natura et opere munitum.** This place is probably to be identified with the fortress of Bigbury, which lies on a wooded hill two miles west of Canterbury. It was built shortly before the invasions of Caesar and was the largest Belgic fortress south of the Thames, being protected not only by the natural slope of the hill, but also by a rampart and a ditch.

19. **testudine facta et aggere ad munitiones adiecto.** The *testudo* (='tortoise') was a mobile covering used to protect troops engaged in attacking walls, filling up ditches, etc. It might be a wooden pent-house moving on wheels, or it might be formed, as in the present instance, by locking shields together. The soldiers of the front rank held their shields in front of them as a vertical screen, while the following ranks held theirs horizontally above their heads. If the men kept close enough together to avoid gaps between the shields, an artificial roof was thus formed against a shower of hostile weapons.

agger here means, not 'rampart,' but 'piled earth.'

There were three stages in the normal Roman method of storming a fortress: (i) the slingers and archers first tried to dislodge the defenders from the walls by discharging their missiles; (ii) the legionaries then charged (under the protection of a *testudo,* if necessary), filled in ditches, and scaled the walls by means of ladders or, as on this occasion, by piling earth against them; (iii) once an entry had been effected, a gate was opened and the main body of troops admitted.

For a more elaborate method, involving both siege and assault, see ch. XLII.

21. **eos fugientis . . . prosequi.** *eos* is ambiguous: it may refer to the men of the 7th Legion or to the Britons. In the latter case, beware of translating *eos fugientis* as 'those fleeing,' an idea which would be rendered by *fugientis* alone. If taken with *eos, fugientis* has a causal or temporal force.

X

2. **in expeditionem.** Do not translate 'on an expedition,' for the Latin is more precise and technical than that. *expeditio* means a task assigned to *expediti* (see note on ch. II, line 15). A neat translation is 'sent as flying columns' (tr. Edwards, *Loeb Classical Library,* p. 247).

4. **extremi,** *i.e.* when only the rearguard of Caesar's column was still in sight.

XI

6. **fabros,** skilled smiths or engineers. They fought in the ranks and were not enrolled in a special corps, but when their services were required they were called out and placed under the command of officers called *praefecti fabrum.*

12. **una munitione.** It has been calculated that a rectangle measuring roughly 1400 by 150 yards would be required for the purpose.

13. **ad laborem.** The *ad* expresses the idea of purpose, 'with a view to.' The phrase must be translated rather freely, *e.g.* 'no interruption being allowed in the work of the troops even in the night-time.'

20. **Cassivellauno.** See Index of Proper Names.

22. **milia passuum LXXX.,** *i.e.* from the sea, where Caesar landed, to the point at which he crossed the Thames, possibly at Brentford (see note on ch. XVIII, line 3).

23. **cum reliquis civitatibus,** especially with his neighbours, the Trinobantes, who lived in Essex (see note on ch. XX).

XII

Some scholars have regarded this chapter and the two which follow as an interpolation, and it is suggested that the description of Britain which they contain was compiled by an unknown reporter for Caesar's use and then found its way into the text. Certainty on such a matter is impossible.

4. **eis nominibus civitatum appellantur,** *e.g.* the Atrebates, a tribe found both in Belgium and in South Britain, though the latter branch of it is not mentioned by Caesar. The construction of this sentence is loose, since *quibus* refers to *civitatum*, while its correlative *eis* is coupled with *nominibus*.

7. **agros colere coeperunt.** Previous inhabitants of Britain had attached themselves to those parts of the country where the soil was light, naturally drained, and free from forest. (Pl. I). The Belgae began to clear the forests and to cultivate the heavier soils. They introduced the villa-system (*cf.* line 8, *creberrima aedificia*), sprinkling the countryside with farm-houses of a type that was to remain typical of British agriculture till the end of the Roman period.

10. **Utuntur . . . pro nummo.** This is an ungainly sentence and the text is not above suspicion. As it stands it seems to imply that Caesar found in Britain three forms of currency: (i) bronze—in a form other than coins, possibly ingots; (ii) gold coins; (iii) iron bars. This would agree with the archaeological evidence which suggests that the oldest coins found in the island are gold and that copper and silver came later.

It is likely that the use of coinage was introduced into Britain by the Belgae, though it is not certain that coins were actually struck in the country before Caesar's invasion. Caesar's words do not imply that the coins which he saw were produced on the spot, and they may have been imported from Gaul. Most of the pre-Roman coins found in this country are uninscribed, and their place of origin is unknown, but it is clear that they passed current over a wide area. The types which occur on these coins were derived from classical models—more specifically from the coins of Philip of Macedon, which were the first to penetrate deeply into the Celtic world—though they became almost unrecognisable in course of time (Pl. II, *b*, i).

Numerous objects resembling half-finished swords have been found in the south-west counties, and these are generally assumed to be examples of the *taleae ferreae* to which Caesar refers. They are not found among the Belgae of the south-east, in whose territory real coins are most abundant, and seem to represent a form of currency used by the Celtic tribes of the south-west before coins were introduced (Pl. II, *a*).

12. **in mediterraneis regionibus.** Actually tin was found in Cornwall, which in Caesar's time was the source of most of the tin used in western Europe and the Mediterranean, but the secret of its origin was carefully guarded and Caesar mistakenly says that it came from the 'inland regions,' though he probably meant little more than 'from a distance.' A generation later Caesar's adopted son, Augustus, opened up the tin-mines of Spain, and this proved a severe blow to the Cornish industry.

13. **in maritimis ferrum.** The chief source of iron was the Weald of Sussex (whose iron mines were not finally abandoned till the nineteenth century), and it is to this region that Caesar is referring here, but the frequent and widespread discovery by archaeologists of iron objects of the first century B.C. suggests that iron was easy to come by in many parts.

14. **aere utuntur importato.** *aes* here means either copper or bronze, the alloy of copper and tin, and the context shows that what is intended is the metal, not objects

made from it. Copper is found in Britain, but there is no evidence that it was mined before Caesar's time. Yet bronze objects were certainly produced, and it is quite possible that the British bronze foundries drew their tin from native sources and their copper from abroad.

15. **praeter fagum atque abietem.** There is some mistake here. The beech (*fagus*) was certainly to be found in Britain before the Romans landed, though the silver fir (*abies*) is not indigenous and had not then been imported. Three explanations of Caesar's statement have been offered: (i) he was mistaken about the beech; (ii) by *fagus* he meant, not beech, but some other kind of tree; (iii) *praeter* means, not 'except,' but 'besides,' and *abies* means not 'silver fir,' but 'fir' in general, and thus Caesar meant 'there is timber of all sorts besides the beech and fir,' implying that these were the commonest. This, however, is not true, so we must adopt either the first or the second explanation.

16. **Leporem et gallinam et anserem.** The passage suggests that these were sacred animals.

XIII

2. **contra Galliam.** Caesar thought that the coast of Gaul, from the Rhine to the Pyrenees, was parallel with the south coast of Britain. His remark in line 6 that the west side of Britain faces Spain is thus intelligible.

8. **transmissus** is genitive, depending on *spatio*, 'with the same length of crossing as.'

10. **Mona.** The Isle of Man must be meant here (*in hoc medio cursu*), though Anglesea had the same name.

12. **non nulli scripserunt,** *e.g.* Pytheas of Massilia, a traveller who came to Britain in the fourth century B.C. and apparently got the impression that the islands off the north coast lay near the Arctic Circle.

14. **certis ex aqua mensuris,** *i.e.* measurements taken with the water-clock (clepsydra). Caesar's meaning is that, if the summer nights were shorter than in Italy, the winter nights could be assumed to be longer, and thus, to

this extent, his own observations confirmed those of previous writers.

19. **eius angulus lateris,** *i.e.* Kent.

XIV

4. **frumenta non serunt . . . pellibusque sunt vestiti.** Caesar was misinformed. Corn was grown by the remoter and less civilised tribes even in the Bronze Age, and the discovery of numerous spindle-whorls of stone, bone, and baked clay shows that they wove woollen and linen clothes.

lacte et carne, instrumental.

6. **Omnes . . . se Britanni vitro inficiunt.** Casear's descriptions of blue-stained barbarians is only half of the picture. To judge from archaelogical finds, the chieftains must have been splendidly and imposingly equipped. The horses which drew their chariots had harness adorned with open-work bronze ornaments and bridle-bits with enamelled cheek-pieces; they themselves fastened their cloaks with coral-studded brooches and wore richly decorated scabbards and shields of polished bronze with designs picked out in enamel (Pl. III). These objects have been frequently found by excavation, and their artistic merit is high.

10. **deni duodenique,** *i.e.* 'groups of 10 or 12.' Caesar seems to be ascribing this custom to the Britons as a whole, though other ancient writers (*e.g.* Strabo and Dio Cassius) ascribe it only to remote districts. The custom did not exist among Celtic tribes, and it is likely that here again Caesar was misinformed.

XV

The narrative is resumed from the end of ch. XI. During the ten days that Caesar spent on the coast, the military situation had changed. After the fall of Bigbury, which seems to have been the most important city south of the Thames, the Kentish chiefs decided to invoke the aid of Cassivellaunus (ch. XI), who was made commander-in-chief and, presumably, brought an army from his own kingdom in Hertfordshire. When Caesar recommenced operations, he felt the influence of this new personality and realised what the Britons could do when well led. He saw that the only hope of victory was to strike at Cassivellaunus' territory across the Thames.

6. **intermisso spatio,** 'after an interval.'

11. **atque eis primis legionum duarum,** the first, and therefore (by Roman organisation) the best cohort in each legion.

16. **tribunus militum.** See Introduction, p. 24.

XVI

4. **cedentis,** 'a retreating enemy.'

neque ab signis discedere auderent, tr. 'they dare not abandon their close formation.' The *signa* were important as rallying-points for the troops, and the word can hardly be translated literally (see Introduction, p. 23).

9. **ex essedis desilirent.** The native British forces consisted of infantry and charioteers, and there was no cavalry in the strict sense. The charioteers might be used in two ways: (i) as a kind of cavalry, manoeuvring about the battlefield and discharging their weapons from the chariots. Caesar's account of his first expedition shows that they acquired extraordinary skill in this type of manoeuvre (Book IV, ch. XXXIII); (ii) as mobile infantry, fighting in conjunction with the cavalry. In this case, they came up between the squadrons, bearing a fighter and a driver. The fighter then dismounted and fought on foot, while the driver and chariot waited nearby to pick him up, when necessary. According to Tacitus, who wrote an account of Roman Britain during the first century A.D., the drivers were of nobler birth than the fighters, who were retainers.

It was a practice among some Celtic tribes to bury warrior-chiefs with their weapons and portions of chariots. Many of these graves have been excavated in Gaul and some in Britain, and remains of chariots have been found in them (Introduction, p. 1). We gather from Livy that in 295 B.C., during the Samnite wars, Gallic chariots routed Roman cavalry, but as a weapon of war they had passed out of use in Gaul before Caesar conquered the country, and he nowhere mentions them in connection with his wars with the Gallic tribes. Their use, however, still continued in Britain, where it had been introduced from Gaul—notably among the Parisii, a tribe that lived in the East Riding of Yorkshire and had probably migrated from the Seine valley (Introduction, p. 6).

The British chariots were light in structure—the diameters of their wheels varied between 2 ft. 4½ in. and 2 ft. 11 in.—and could be pulled by small horses. Their place in Gaul had been taken by cavalry, and it has been suggested that the change was due to the importation of a new breed of horses, big and powerful enough to carry a man into battle. Previously in Gaul, and still in Caesar's time in Britain, the horses were small, unequal to carrying a heavy rider, though able to pull a light car.

The parts of the chariots which are found in the chariot-graves are iron tires from the wheels, bronze hoops which bound the naves, bronze bridle-bits, and bronze terets for the reins (Pl. IV). It is commonly thought that these chariots were armed with scythes, but Caesar does not say so: the best ancient writers agree with him, and no scythes have been found in the chariot-graves.

10. **equestris autem proeli ratio . . . inferebat.** This sentence is difficult and many editors consider it spurious. If it is genuine, it must refer to the combined cavalry and chariot tactics of the Britons, which Caesar found very difficult to combat. *equestris proeli ratio* has been variously explained: (i) a loose phrase for the British manner of fighting ('their cavalry tactics'); (ii) 'the general nature of the combat,' *i.e.* between Roman cavalry on the one hand and British cavalry and chariots on the other; (iii) 'regular cavalry tactics,' *i.e.* those normally used by the Romans. Certainty is impossible. *cedentibus et insequentibus* seems to refer to Caesar's cavalry.

13. **stationesque dispositas haberent.** *stationes* cannot here mean 'outposts' or 'piquets,' which do not suit the context. Caesar is describing the manner in which the Britons stationed their reserves. Tr. 'detachments.'

XVII

5. **cum C. Trebonio legato.** For the *legati*, see Introduction, p. 24, and for C. Trebonius, see Index of Proper Names.

7. **sic uti ab signis legionibusque non absisterent,** *i.e.* they even attacked the legions drawn up for battle. Caesar remembered that the 7th Legion had been surprised while foraging the previous year (Bk. IV, ch. XXXII), though the British chariots were powerless against a legion in battle-formation; so he made his plan accordingly. The foragers lured the Britons on to the rest of the troops, drawn up in mass. For the *signa*, see Introduction, p. 23.

XVIII

3. **uno omnino loco . . . transiri potest.** The place where Caesar crossed the Thames has not been determined. Arguments have been advanced in favour of two places, viz. Cowey Stakes, near Walton-on-Thames, and Brentford. Caesar's statement that it was the only spot where the Thames could be crossed on foot must not be taken as applying to the whole length of the river, but only to that part of it which bordered the territory of Cassivellaunus. Even so, the statement is incorrect.

9. **praemisso equitatu confestim legiones subsequi iussit.** *praemittere* means 'to send in advance,' but this sentence can hardly mean that Caesar first sent the cavalry across the river and then ordered the infantry to follow in their wake—an operation which seems impossible in view of the stakes and the waiting Britons. Possibly the cavalry were sent round to a flank where there were no stakes, and the infantry crossed while the attention of the Britons was distracted.

XIX

12. **relinquebatur ut . . . poterant.** 'the only course left was that Caesar. . . .' *discedi* and *noceretur* are impersonal passives.

The Roman cavalry, not being able to deal with the chariots when unsupported by infantry, could not be sent too far afield for fear of being attacked, so that their movements were governed by the marching capacity of the infantry which protected them (*labore atque itinere, i.e.* work consisting in marching). Tr. 'to injure the enemy as much as the marching powers of the legionaries would allow.'

XX

1. **Trinobantes.** See Index of Proper Names. The previous hostilities between the Trinobantes and Cassivellaunus were part of the continuous wars which that ambitious chief fought with his neighbours (ch. XI). The king of the Trinobantes had been killed by Cassivellaunus, but his son, Mandubracius, managed to escape. He took refuge with Caesar in Gaul and accompanied him on this expedition. The overtures from the Trinobantes which are described in this chapter came just in time, since, as we saw in ch. XIX, Caesar's cavalry had been prevented from foraging and gathering the grain on which he was relying. Hence to the usual demand for hostages he added a demand for corn. Mandubracius was rewarded with the kingship of his people, in which position he would be a useful check on Cassivellaunus.

XXI

2. **Cenimagni, Segontiaci, Ancalites, Bibroci, Cassi.** The names of four of these tribes are otherwise unknown; that of the Segontiaci is found on coins. The chief value of their surrender to Caesar was that he discovered from them the position of Cassivellaunus' capital, which his enemy had cleverly managed to keep from him till then.

4. **oppidum Cassivellauni.** This fortress, whose name Caesar nowhere mentions, is probably that which can still be traced on a hill-top near Wheathampstead, about 5 miles north of St Albans (Pl. X, *a*). Its area was at least 100 acres, and it was protected by an earthwork, composed of a ditch, 40 feet deep, with a high bank on each side, the inner bank being considerably higher than the outer. The

fortress was partly excavated in 1932, and numerous objects were found in it—a loom weight, a clay spindle-whorl, an iron knife, a pair of bronze tweezers, a bronze brooch, and innumerable pieces of pottery—all dating from about the time of Caesar's invasion. Near the *oppidum*, between the valleys of the Lea and the Ver, was another earthwork of the same date, again composed of a ditch with banks, but this time running more or less in a straight line. It seems to have been the north-west frontier of Cassivellaunus' kingdom, serving partly to mark the boundary clearly, partly to prevent cattle-raiding.

7. **cum silvas . . . vallo atque fossa munierunt.** This description does not, of course, suit all ancient British fortresses. Those in Dorset and Wiltshire, for example, are situated on hills that can never have been thickly wooded because the soil is too light and thin. It was characteristic of the Belgae to build their hill-forts in the forests (Introduction, p. 7). Thus the hill of the Wheathampstead fortress is said by the excavator to be 'mostly capped by a cold and sticky boulder-clay which must have been cleared of a fairly dense woodland by the original occupiers' (*Antiquity*, March 1933, p. 27).

XXII

5. **eis imperat.** Though Cassivellaunus had been deserted by many of his allies and had lost his capital, his authority was such that he could persuade three Kentish chiefs to try and carry out his plan. The attack on the naval camp near Deal was a clever move that threatened Caesar's communications and his safety. Caesar fails to mention that he himself visited the camp in connexion with it, but on Aug. 5 he wrote a letter from the coast to the orator Cicero, and the most likely cause of his presence there at that time was the attack which Cassivellaunus conceived and these four Kentish chiefs carried out.

12. **per Atrebatem Commium.** Commius had been set over the Gallic branch of the Atrebates by Caesar as a client king. As there were Atrebates in Britain (Berkshire)

as well as in Gaul, he was no doubt considered influential on both sides of the Channel, and at the outset of the first invasion of Britain he was sent to use his influence with the Britons on Caesar's behalf. Their immediate response to his overtures was to put him under arrest. Caesar, however, secured his release, and he and his escort of thirty horsemen later did Caesar good service. His subsequent career proves his influence in Britain, for, after falling foul of Caesar in the rebellion of 52 B.C., he fled to Britain and we find him striking coins in Hampshire (Pl. II, *b*, iii).

How did Commius and Cassivellaunus come to be in touch with one another on this occasion? Caesar was sometimes guilty of misrepresentation in his Commentaries, and there are those who think that on this occasion he himself tried to expedite negotiations in view of the disturbed state of Gaul. It had been his original intention to winter in Britain, but the sudden risings in Gaul made him change his plan. He must have been anxious to leave Britain with some appearance of victory, and it is suggested that he himself sent Commius to Cassivellaunus, for although the latter was beaten, he might carry on a guerilla campaign for what remained of the summer.

17. **quid in annos singulos vectigalis . . . penderet.** It is not known whether Cassivellaunus actually paid any tribute, but, as he seems to have obeyed the third condition (that he should not harm Mandubracius and the Trinobantes), it is quite likely that he did pay it for a time. During the principate of Augustus, the Britons were not required to furnish tribute, but they paid duties on goods entering and leaving Gallic harbours, and these duties may have been substituted for tribute when the Romans found that the conquest of Britain had to be postponed indefinitely. Caesar's remark was doubtless intended to convey to the Romans that a new province had been added to their empire.

XXIII

9. **remitterentur, et . . . et . . .** The *re-* in *remitterentur* applies strictly to the ships of the first relay, which disembarked their troops and returned for more, but not to

those of Labienus, which had not yet crossed to Britain. Though loose, however, the expression is intelligible.

The first expedition to Britain had been honoured with a public thanksgiving in Rome, but no such distinction is mentioned after the second invasion. Perhaps hopes had been raised too high, and the conquest of at least a portion of the island had been expected. Actually, however, as Professor Collingwood has shown, the results achieved, though they fell short of conquest, were not meagre: (i) from the military point of view, Caesar had learnt how to deal successfully with the British war-chariots, and he had destroyed two large fortresses of the tribes with which he fought; (ii) from the political point of view, he had left a client king ruling over the important tribe of the Trinobantes, and all the tribes with which he had come into contact had—sooner or later—submitted and undertaken to pay tribute; (iii) from the financial point of view, he had been less successful. He had taken back with him a large number of slaves, but he had learnt little or nothing about the economic possibilities of the island. In spite of this, however, Caesar himself, if not the people in Rome, might regard the results which he achieved as boding well for the future conquest of the island (Collingwood and Myres, *Roman Britain and the English Settlements*, pp. 51–52).

XXIV

1. **concilioque Gallorum . . . peracto.** See note on ch. II, line 16.

6. **C. Fabio legato,** etc. All these officers, except M. Crassus and L. Roscius, are either stated to be, or known from other sources to be, *legati* (see Introduction, p. 24). M. Crassus was *quaestor* and the position of L. Roscius is doubtful (see note on ch. LIII, line 23).

The provincial quaestor looked after the financial business and commissariat. He had charge of the money-chest from which the expenses of the administration were disbursed and into which taxes were paid. Theoretically, the quaestors should have been assigned to the various provinces by lot, but Caesar and other powerful generals did not always abide by this formality. Caesar too, as here, employed quaestors for military purposes.

7. For information about these tribes, see the Index of Proper Names. As often with Gallic tribes, the names of some of them have been preserved in that of their former capital, *e.g.* the Remi survive in Rheims, and the Treveri in Trèves. We learn elsewhere that the quarters of Trebonius were at Samarobriva (Amiens) and those of Sabinus and Cotta at Aduatuca.

10. **in † Belgis.†** We gather from ch. XLVI that Crassus was stationed among the Bellovaci.

13. **cohortis V.** It is known that Caesar had 9 legions in all at this time, yet he only accounts for 8 and a half. Possibly the odd 5 cohorts were the nucleus of a ninth legion which had been depleted to fill those which had lost men by death or disease.

22. **milibus passuum centum continebantur.** These words can only mean that the camps were included within a circuit of 100 miles, which is incorrect, since, for example, the quarters of Sabinus and Cotta among the Eburones were more than 100 miles from those of Trebonius at Samarobriva. To explain the words as meaning that no camp was more than 100 miles from some one other is forcing the Latin. Possibly something has gone wrong with the numeral in the manuscript.

XXV

During the winter which followed, the Gallic tribes made a series of attacks on certain of the legionary camps, and the military skill of Caesar and his *legati* was tried to the utmost. Labienus managed to nip the rebellion amongst the Treviri in the bud, but Sabinus and Cotta lost their lives and Cicero was rescued by Caesar only in the nick of time. The attacks were the prelude to a new phase in Caesar's conquest of Gaul, marked not, as in the first three years of his campaigns, by pitched battles between his armies and the Gallic peoples, but by long sieges, desperately withstood by tribes who hoped by concerted rebellion to escape the Roman yoke that was descending upon them.

1. **Erat in Carnutibus . . . Tasgetius . . .** See the Index of Proper Names. For Caesar's use of client kings, see note on ch. VI, line 7. In ch. III we had another example of trouble caused by rivalry among Gallic chieftains.

5. **Tertium iam hunc annum regnantem . . . interfecerunt.** The text in this passage is corrupt and, as it stands, is nonsense. One editor believes that a clause has been lost, while some manuscripts read *inimici iam palam multis ex civitate auctoribus interfecerunt*, meaning that Tasgetius became so unpopular with his own people that there was much open opposition to him, and his enemies killed him.

8. **ad pluris pertinebat.** For the use of the comparative, see note on ch. VII, line 4.

9. **L. Plancum . . . proficisci iubet.** This still left C. Trebonius, a *legatus*, and M. Crassus, a quaestor, in Belgium with two legions.

13. **ab omnibus legatis quaestoribusque.** See note on ch. XXIV, line 6. The word *quaestoribus* has caused difficulties, since, strictly speaking, there should have been one quaestor only in the province. Apart from this chapter, the other passages in which Caesar seems to imply that there was more than one quaestor can be explained away (*e.g.* ch. LIII, line 23). We must conclude either that Caesar for some reason had more than one quaestor or that there is something wrong with the text in this chapter.

15. **locumque hibernis esse munitum.** *hibernis* must be dative, 'the place for the winter-quarters,' but it is a surprising usage and some editors omit the word.

Roman military encampments were of three kinds: (i) temporary camps, intended for one or two nights only; (ii) semi-permanent camps, suitable for occupation during a whole season (Pl. XI); (iii) permanent camps or forts. All tended to follow the same general plan, but differed in the strength and durability of their fortifications and buildings, and in the spaciousness of their accommodation (see note on ch. XLIII, line 3). The plan was rectangular, and the area, even when the site was occupied for only a single night, was surrounded by a ditch (*fossa*) and a rampart (*agger*) supporting a palisade (*vallum*). In temporary camps the rampart was of earth and the palisade of stakes, of which each legionary carried two. In more permanent structures, the rampart might be of turf and might have a timber lining in front, with a more elaborate palisade. Sometimes the timber lining was continued up to form a parapet and battlements, thus doing away with the need for a palisade. In forts the rampart might be of concrete, faced with brick or stone, with parapet and battlements of the same material. The internal arrangements differed from one period to another, but the main feature of the layout was a network of streets based on two axes which crossed one another at right angles. In the centre of the camp, near the intersection of the two axes, was the general's headquarters (*praetorium*) and an open space (*forum*) for purposes of meeting and parade.

XXVI

2. **repentini tumultus ac defectionis.** There is little doubt that one of the reasons for this revolt was the resentment which the Gauls felt against Roman exactions and especially against their practice of billeting troops for the winter in or near their cities. Wherever in the empire such billeting took place, it was very unpopular. In the East wealthy cities paid large sums to avoid it, and we learn from Plutarch that, in Spain, twenty years before, the rebel Roman general Sertorius had gained much popularity with the inhabitants for stopping the practice.

3. **ab Ambiorige et Catuvolco.** See ch. XXIV, line 15.

cum ad fines . . . comportavissent, *i.e.* they had attended on the frontiers of their kingdom to pay their respects to the two Roman generals and had furnished supplies for their troops.

5. **Indutiomari Treveri nuntiis.** Indutiomarus was burning with indignation for the action which Caesar took in his dispute with Cingetorix (ch. IV). Caesar had exacted 200 hostages from him, among whom were his son and all his kinsmen. But Indutiomarus' action at this time seems to suggest that his hands were not tied, and possibly Caesar had set the hostages free on his return from Britain.

Think what *nuntiis* means—'messengers' or 'messages'?

10. **Hispanis equitibus.** This is the sole mention of Spanish horsemen in Caesar's Gallic army, though we have already found him importing material from Spain to equip his fleet (ch. I, line 15), and later in the war he obtained horses from Spain (Book VII, ch. LV). He had been governor there in 61 B.C. (Introduction, p. 12), and doubtless still had many connexions with the country.

12. **suo more conclamaverunt.** The point is that the Romans would not have shouted, but would have sent a representative.

XXVII

5. **pro Caesaris in se beneficiis.** Caesar conquered the Aduatuci in 57 B.C. and treated them with great severity. His service to Ambiorix probably dates from that time. Doubtless he had hoped by generous treatment to make Ambiorix a loyal client.

11. **neque id quod fecerit,** etc. Notice the way in which the tenses of the subjunctive are used in the long piece of *oratio obliqua* that forms the rest of this chapter. In lines 5–25, the tenses are rightly historic, except *fecerit* (line 11), *potuerit* (line 17), and *confidat* (line 19), while from line 25 to the end they are primary. Possibly Caesar used *fecerit* and *potuerit* to indicate something that had recently happened as distinct from the other events that Ambiorix is recounting. After line 25, the vividness of the exhortation and the number of present infinitives are enough to account for the irregularity. The sequence of tenses is based on sense rather than strict rule.

13. **suaque esse eiusmodi imperia.** Actually the 'masses' had very little influence on politics, management of which lay in the hands of the nobles. It seems either that Ambiorix was lying or that *multitudo* means here not the 'mass of the people' but the 'body of landowners.'

25. **pro pietate,** 'as the claims of his country required'; see Vocabulary.

27. **pro hospitio.** See note on ch. VI, line 10. Tianslate 'in view of their friendship.'

30. **Ipsorum esse consilium, velintne,** *i.e.* 'it was for the Romans themselves to consider, whether . . .'

32. **ad Ciceronem aut ad Labienum.** The camp of Sabinus and Cotta was at Aduatuca, the site of which, despite some diversity of opinion, is probably to be found near Tongres in Belgium (see note on ch. xxxii, line 6). Cicero's camp has been placed at Binche, on the Sambre, and that of Labienus at Mouzon, on the Meuse. If these identifications are correct, the distance of Sabinus and Cotta from Cicero was not 50 miles, but nearly 70.

XXVIII

7. **ad consilium rem deferunt.** Where was the council of war held? In ch. xxx, line 4, we are told that when Sabinus raised his voice he could be heard by a large part of the soldiers. It might seem at first sight that the council was held in the open air and that the soldiers were massed in the open space in front of the general's headquarters. But we must remember that the month was October, that the discussion was prolonged till midnight (ch. xxxi, line 6), and that the camp was a permanent or semi-permanent one and there must have been some sort of hall suitable for a council of war. It looks as if discipline was already getting slack and the soldiers were crowding round the doors.

9. **tribuni militum . . . centuriones.** For the *tribuni militum,* see Introduction, p. 24. The *primorum ordinum centuriones* are either the six centurions of the first cohort in a legion (see diagram on p. 22), or the centurions of the first century in each cohort, or both. Probably the first alternative is correct (Parker, *Roman Legions*, p. 34).

11. **quantasvis magnas etiam copias.** Something has gone wrong with the text here, since *quantasvis* and *magnas* cannot stand together and *etiam* seems out of place. One editor suggests the insertion of *Gallorum* after *quantasvis* ('as many Gallic troops as you like and a good number of German troops too'), while another simplifies the sense by reading *quantasvis copias etiam* ('even German forces,

however numerous'). In explanation of *etiam* we must remember that the Romans never conquered the Germans and doubtless regarded them as more formidable foes than the Gauls.

13. **rem esse testimonio, quod . . .**, 'experience proved this; for . . .' (Rice Holmes).

14. **ultro,** 'actually,' 'into the bargain.' They not only repelled the attack, but did damage as well.

18. **quam auctore hoste . . . capere consilium.** Note the order of words, 'than to follow the advice of an enemy in . . .'

XXIX

5. **Caesarem arbitrari profectum in Italiam;** understand *se* and think who is the subject of *arbitrari. Italia* here means Cisalpine Gaul.

7. **si ille adesset . . . venturos fuisse.** Strict syntax would require *adfuisset* and *venturos fuisse,* but sense overrides syntactical usage, since *Carnutes . . . fuisse capturos* refers to a more remote event than *Eburones . . . venturos esse.*

9. **non . . . spectare,** *sc. sese.*

11. **Ariovisti mortem.** See Introduction, p. 11. After his defeat, Ariovistus escaped from the Roman cavalry by crossing the Rhine in a boat (Book I, ch. LIII). His death is not elsewhere recorded by Caesar.

16. **Suam sententiam . . . esse tutam,** 'his own view made for safety in either case.'

17. **durius.** See note on ch. VII, line 4.

XXX

2. **a Cotta primisque ordinibus,** i.e. *a primorum ordinum centurionibus.* 'Similarly in English one of the musicians in an orchestra is called "the first violin"' (Rice Holmes).

9. **non reiecti . . . intereant,** 'instead of perishing, abandoned and exiled . . .'

XXXI

1. **comprehendunt,** *i.e.* 'the officers seize the two generals by the hand.'

7. **permotus,** 'though much disturbed.'

12. **Omnia excogitantur, quare . . . augeatur.** They felt uneasy about the decision to march and for that reason invented excuses to justify it. They pointed out the danger of remaining where they were and the way in which that danger would be increased by the need for long and exhausting watches. There is an undertone of censure running all through this chapter.

14. **ex castris proficiscuntur . . .** Which direction did they take? Of the two alternatives mentioned in ch. XXVII, line 32, the camp of Labienus seems the likelier, since that was where the few survivors made for (ch. XXXVII, line 18).

ut quibus esset persuasum, 'like men convinced that . . .' The subjunctive is causal.

17. **longissimo agmine maximisque impedimentis.** Caesar is hinting at the criminal negligence of Sabinus, who did not even take the obvious precaution of keeping his troops close together so that, if attacked, it would be easy to form battle array, and of making them march as lightly equipped as possible.

XXXII

6. **in magnam convallem.** The site of the Roman camp is thought to have been at or near Tongres. The valley in which they were ambushed would seem to be the valley of the Geer. It is known from other sources that the hills to the south of Tongres were covered with forest in ancient times.

XXXIII

1. **Titurius, qui nihil ante providisset . . .** What is the point of the subjunctive?

3. **ut,** 'in such a way that.'

11. **per se,** 'in person.'

13. **iusserunt pronuntiare.** In English we should normally use a passive infinitive, and this can also be used in Latin (ch. XXXIV, line 11). With the active, compare the French use: *il fit proclamer.*

14. **in orbem consisterent,** *i.e.* form a hollow square and fight outwards.

20. **ab signis.** See Introduction, p. 23.

XXXIV

5. **Erant et virtute et † numero pugnandi † pares.** As it stands, the text does not make sense. Possibly the sentence is better omitted, though *studio* has been suggested instead of *numero.* The narrative makes it clear that the Romans were *not* numerically equal to the Eburones.

7. **a fortuna.** The use of the preposition gives to *fortuna* a personal quality. The goddess Fortuna was a Roman object of worship.

13. **levitate armorum.** See Introduction, p. 4.

14. **noceri:** impersonal passive.

XXXV

4. **ab latere aperto,** the right side. Why?

9. **conferti,** 'in close array.' Used of troops in battle-formation.

12. **ad horam octavum,** *i.e.* till between 2 and 3 p.m. The Romans divided the period of daylight into 12 hours, which varied in length according to the time of the year.

14. **qui . . . primum pilum duxerat.** See diagram on p. 22. He had been the senior centurion of his legion. Notice the respect with which Caesar speaks of his centurions both here and in ch. XLIV (see Introduction, p. 23). We are not told why Balventius had ceased to hold his office, but he may have been one of the *evocati*—men who had served their full time and remained with their leader as volunteers.

16. **tragula.** See note on ch. XLVIII, line 11.

XXXVI

3. **Cn. Pompeium.** This interpreter, we may presume, was a provincial, probably a Gaul, who had been given the Roman citizenship and had taken the family name of his Roman patron. It is suggested that he received the citizenship from Pompey the Great during the war which he fought against Sertorius in Spain (76–72 B.C.).

5. **sperare,** *sc. se.*

8. **Ille cum Cotta . . . communicat,** 'communicates with Cotta, and suggests that (*ut*), if he thinks fit (*si videatur*), etc.'

11. **Cotta . . . perseverat.** Cotta all through is represented as the chary commander, Sabinus as the fool.

XXXVII

1. **Sabinus . . . se sequi iubet . . .** Sabinus is represented as the senior of the two commanders, and, when they are mentioned in conjunction, his name comes first (ch. XXIV, line 16, and ch. XXVI, line 4). In ch. XXXIX, line 5, the disaster is referred to by his name alone. As they had a legion and five cohorts with them, possibly he had command of the legion and Cotta that of the five cohorts.

16. **ad unum omnes . . . se ipsi interficiunt . . .,** 'they killed one another to a man.' The loss of some 5000 men was indeed a great disaster, and the whole episode might have cost Caesar his province. Yet he writes with great restraint, criticising Sabinus by implication and not by express statement, and at the same time mentioning by name those whose valour was outstanding. Suetonius tells how, on hearing of the disaster, Caesar let his hair and beard grow till he had avenged it.

XXXVIII

2. **in Aduatucos . . . proficiscitur.** See map on pp. 14–15. He marches westwards in the direction of Cicero's camp, probably along the valleys of the Meuse and the Sambre.

6. **sui . . . liberandi . . .** *sui* is plural here, but as the form is the same as that of the singular, *liberandi* is attracted into the singular for euphony.

XXXIX

1. **ad Ceutrones,** etc. These peoples are doubtless *pagi* of the Nervii (see Introduction, p. 3), but they are nowhere else mentioned, and Caesar doubtless mentions them with a certain complacency to stress the size of the rebellion.

4. **ad Ciceronis hiberna advolant . . .,** thought to have been at Binche on the R. Sambre (see note on ch. LIII, line 3). Notice the emphatic position of the ablative absolute which follows. We may translate by 'before' and a temporal clause.

6. **Huic quoque accidit, quod fuit necesse.** Caesar shows the similarity between the case of Cicero and that of Sabinus (ch. XXVI, line 7), but he hastens to say that no blame attaches to Cicero (*quod fuit necesse*).

14. **adepti** here stands for a condition, 'if they won this victory.'

XL

1. **Mittuntur ad Caesarem,** *i.e.* to Samarobriva (Amiens), the headquarters of the legion of C. Trebonius.

2. **si pertulissent,** *i.e.* if the messengers got them through.

5. **turres admodum centum xx . . .** The towers were built of wood, with several storeys, and from them missiles could be showered on the enemy. They played a prominent part in Roman siege-works and, when used as here for defence, they were in a light and temporary form the counterparts of the wall-towers that are found in the fortifications of many Roman cities.

Rice Holmes points out that at Alesia, where Caesar used similar towers, they were spaced 80 feet apart and that, allowing for the same intervals here, the perimetre of Cicero's camp could not have been less than two miles. The area would then be 160 acres, much too large for a single legion, which could hardly take more than 50 acres.

It may be that the number given for the towers is wrong or that they were placed closer together than 80 feet. One editor suggests that the towers were connected by platforms, and, if this was so, they cannot have been 80 feet apart.

6. **quae deesse operi videbantur,** *i.e.* the apparent deficiencies in the earthworks.

8. **fossam complent.** See note on ch. xxv, line 15.

10. **ad laborem.** See note on ch. xi, line 13.

14. **multae praeustae sudes,** etc. The stakes were burnt to a hard point, and the 'mural pikes' were heavier than the normal kind and suitable for hurling from walls or towers.

15. **turres contabulantur,** etc. Various interpretations have been placed on *contabulantur* = 'raised stage by stage,' 'raised a stage,' 'furnished with storeys.' Whatever the precise meaning, the general form of the towers is clear. They consisted of a series of storeys, each with its own platform on which troops could stand and from which missiles could be hurled down on the enemy. *Pinnae* are 'battlements' or 'pinnacles,' placed on the successive storeys to protect the troops fighting from them, while *loricae* are breastworks hung over the wooden *pinnae* for their protection.

18. **ut ultro . . . cogeretur . . .,** 'he was actually (*ultro*) compelled to spare himself by the protests (*vocibus*) of the soldiers who crowded about him (*concursu*).'

XLI

1. **aliquem sermonis aditum causamque amicitiae,** *i.e.* 'who had some means of getting into conversation with Cicero and reason to call themselves his friends.'

11. **ut nihil nisi hiberna recusent. . . .** On the unpopularity of Roman winter-quarters, see note on ch. xxvi, line 2.

13. **per se,** tr. (in direct speech) 'as far as we are concerned.'

18. **se adiutore utantur,** 'they might use his good offices' (Loeb).

XLII

1. **vallo pedum IX et fossa pedum XV.** The height given for the *vallum* includes both the palisade and the rampart on which it was placed. The proportion 2 : 3 between the height of the vallum and the width of the ditch was followed by Caesar himself (Book II, ch. v). The Romans normally made their ditches V-shaped, with a small square channel at the bottom. This channel made the ditch easier to clean, and also, by compelling an opponent to place his feet parallel to the line of the ditch, made it difficult to climb out.

3. **quos clam . . . captivos:** prisoners from the Roman army whom they kept in secret.

5. **nulla . . . copia:** an ablative absolute.

7. **sagulis.** The *sagulum*, or *sagum*, was a cloak, made of a square piece of cloth which was attached to the right shoulder. It was Celtic in origin (Introduction, p. 4), though it had been adopted by the Romans.

9. **milium (p̃. XV) in circuitu III . . .** The text seems to be faulty. The best manuscripts read *milium p̃* (=*passuum*) *xv in circuitum.* To put a ditch of 15 miles round Cicero's small camp would have been absurd, and it is better to change the *m* of *circuitum* into *iii* (imputing the mistake to a copyist's error) and to omit *p̃ xv* altogether. A circumvallation of three miles is quite possible.

11. **ad altitudinem valli.** *ad* means 'in proportion to,' not 'up to.' To serve their purpose, the towers, which were moved on wheels, would necessarily be higher than the *vallum.*

11. **falces testudinesque.** The *falces* were wooden beams with iron hooks at the ends and were used for dislodging stones and timber from a wall, usually by men working under the shelter of a *testudo* (see note on ch. IX, line 19).

XLIII

2. **ferventis fusili ex argilla glandis.** Various opinions have been expressed about these 'red-hot bullets of soft clay': (i) that they were made of clay, mixed with coal; (ii) that they were of white-hot clay; (iii) that they were of peat, mixed with clay to weight them. Their precise nature must remain in doubt.

3. **in casas, quae . . . erant tectae . . .** In a temporary camp, the troops would be housed in tents: in a semi-permanent camp such as this, the hutments would be of a more durable nature—of wood, doubtless, with thatched roofs (see note on ch. xxv, line 15).

7. **turres testudinesque agere,** 'to bring up their towers and shelters.' For the method of storming a fortress, see note on ch. ix, line 19.

19. **ut se . . . constipaverant . . .,** 'inasmuch as . . .,' or 'since they had pressed right under the very rampart . . .'

XLIV

1. **fortissimi viri, centuriones, qui primis ordinibus appropinquarent.** Notice that in the story which follows it is centurions once more who are picked out for special commendation. In some half-dozen places in the *Commentaries*, centurions are mentioned by name (*e.g.* ch. xxxv). Doubtless the telling of these stories, which must have been well known in Caesar's army, was intended to rouse the interest of his men and stimulate them to do likewise. For *primis ordinibus*, see note on ch. xxviii, line 9, and for the promotion of centurions, see Introduction, p. 23.

8. **tuae pro laude virtutis** seems untranslatable, and instead of *pro laude* one editor suggests *probandae*, 'chance of proving your courage.'

11. **Ne . . . quidem** can hardly mean 'not even' here. It is a strong negative, 'of course . . . not.'

18. **verutum in balteo defigitur.** For the soldier's belt, see Plate VI.

avertit hic casus vaginam, 'dislodged his scabbard.'

26. **in locum . . . inferiorem concidit,** 'fell into a dip in the ground.'

29. **Sic fortuna . . . utrumque versavit.** 'In their eager rivalry [*in contentione et certamine:* hendiadys], Fortune so balanced them that . . .'

XLV

3. **res ad paucitatem defensorum pervenerat,** 'the burden had fallen on a small number of defenders' (Loeb).

13. **ad Caesarem pervenit.** Caesar does not state that he had already left Samarobriva for Italy, though three other writers—Plutarch, Dio Cassius, and Appian—all agree that he had. If so, he can hardly have got far on his way.

XLVI

Of the 8½ legions with which Caesar started the winter, he had lost 1½ in the rising among the Eburones; that of Cicero was besieged among the Nervii; and those of L. Roscius and L. Munatius Plancus were too far away to be of assistance (see line 10). He thus had four legions with which to attempt the rescue of Cicero, but they were scattered: (i) with him at Samarobriva he had that of C. Trebonius; (ii) to the south, among the Bellovaci, was that of M. Crassus; (iii) C. Fabius had a legion among the Morini; (iv) T. Labienus had the fourth among the Remi.

Caesar's plan was that he himself should march with Trebonius' legion and be joined by Fabius on the way. Crassus should move up to Samarobriva, while Labienus should, if possible, make an independent attack on the Nervii from the southeast. Labienus in the event was unable to move, so that Caesar was able to take only two legions to the rescue of Cicero.

1. **hora circiter undecima diei,** about 5 p.m.

5. **cum nuntio,** 'immediately on the arrival of the messenger.'

8. **rei publicae commodo,** an ablative of attendant circumstances; *cf.* 'with advantage' in English. Perhaps

here it is best translated by 'without detriment to the public interest.'

10. **Reliquam partem exercitus . . .,** *i.e.* the legion under L. Roscius among the Esubii, and that under L. Munatius Plancus, which had been stationed first among the Belgae, and then, on the murder of Tasgetius, had been transferred to the Carnutes (chs. XXIV–XXV).

11. **equites circiter quadringentos.** It seems to have been Caesar's practice to levy cavalry from the Gallic tribes in the spring and send them home in the winter. Hence the small number which he was able to collect now. They were doubtless made up chiefly of Spaniards and Germans, though ch. XLVIII, line 7, shows that some of them were Gauls.

XLVII

1. **Hora circiter tertia,** *i.e.* about 8.30 a.m. The season was about the beginning of November.

5. **litteras publicas:** all the multifarious lists and records connected with the legions and with the province, and Caesar's own documents and copies of his dispatches, from which he would write his *Commentaries* (Introduction, p. 18).

15. **rem gestam in Eburonibus,** *i.e.* the loss of the legion and a half under Sabinus and Cotta.

XLVIII

1. **opinione trium legionum deiectus,** *i.e.* 'disappointed in his expectation of having three legions.'

2. **unum communis salutis auxilium,** 'the only means whereby they could all be saved.'

8. **Graecis conscriptam litteris,** *i.e.* in Latin, but written in Greek letters.

11. **tragulam cum epistola ad ammentum deligata.** The *tragula* was a Celtic weapon, thrown by a thong. Napoleon III had experiments made and found that the use of the thong quadrupled the distance thrown.

XLIX

7. **ab se . . . ad eum,** *i.e.* from Cicero to Caesar.

12. **trans vallem et rivum.** The identification of this valley and stream depends on the site assigned to Cicero's camp. If it is correctly placed at Binche, this valley may be the Val d'Estine, 3 miles to the west.

14. **tantulis copiis.** Against the 60,000 Gauls, Caesar had only two legions and a few cavalry. He gives his own number as 7000, so his legions must have been below strength (Introduction, p. 21).

16. **remittendum de celeritate . . .,** 'that he might slacken his pace.'

18. **etsi erant exigua per se.** The camp in itself was small, being intended for scarcely seven thousand men, but by 'narrowing the roads' (*augustiis viarum*) Caesar made it still smaller.

21. **eo consilio ut . . . veniat,** 'with the object of incurring the contempt of.'

L

12. **portasque obstrui,** viz. by piling rows of turf (see ch. LI, line 9).

13. **quam maxime concursari et . . . agi,** impersonal passives.

LI

6. **ante horam tertiam.** See note on ch. XLVII, line 1.

9. **obstructis in speciem portis,** *i.e.* 'barricaded for show.'

11. **vallum manu scindere.** *vallum* is here used in its strict meaning of palisade, whereas in line 3 it meant the rampart as a whole.

LII

2. **neque etiam parvulo detrimento,** etc., 'and he did not see that any opportunity remained of inflicting the slightest loss upon them.'

6. **non decimum quemque,** 'not one in ten.'

9. **Ciceronem . . . collaudat.** Cicero deserved praise, but doubtless Caesar was anxious also to flatter his brother, the famous orator, whose friendship could be of great service to him in Rome.

16. **quod detrimentum . . ., hoc . . .;** correlatives. *quod* in line 18 means 'because.'

18. **beneficio deorum immortalium. . . .** Suetonius tells us that Caesar was never deterred from any enterprise by religious scruples, and there are, in fact, only three places in his writings where he mentions the intervention of the gods. In the present passage, we must remember, he is speaking to impress his troops and in one of the others to impress the Helvetii.

LIII

1. **per Remos,** 'through the agency of the Remi.'

3. **milia passuum abesset circiter LX.** Actually it is eighty miles from Binche to Mouzon, and this is one reason against placing the camps of Cicero and Labienus at these places. On the vagueness of Caesar's geographical information, see Introduction, p. 20.

4. **post horam nonam,** after 3.30 p.m. Notice the speed with which the news travelled—60 miles in less than nine hours. Elsewhere Caesar says, 'Whenever any event of greater note or importance occurs, the Gauls shout it abroad through fields and districts, and then others take it up in turn and pass it on to their next neighbours' (Bk. VII, ch. iii: tr. Loeb).

11. **in hiberna,** *i.e.* amongst the Morini.

cum tribus legionibus, *i.e.* those of Trebonius, Crassus, and Cicero. It was Caesar's custom to spend the winter doing civil business in the peaceful portion of his province (ch. I, line 2), and the fact that on this occasion he stayed with his army shows the serious view he took of the situation.

15. **Nam illo incommodo de Sabini morte perlato,** *i.e.* when the news became known of the disaster in which Sabinus had met his death.

21. **quin,** 'without his receiving.'

23. **ab L. Roscio (quaestore).** See note on ch. xxv, line 13. The word *quaestore* has been explained away by supposing that a scribe copied the *q* of *quem* twice and another copyist then misunderstood it as being an abbreviation of *quaestore.*

26. **Aremoricae,** 'a Celtic word meaning "maritime"' (Rice Holmes).

LIV

2. **alias . . . alias . . .,** adverbs, 'sometimes . . ., other times . . .'

4. **Tamen Senones,** etc. Notice how elaborately, yet carefully and clearly this sentence is constructed. The subject is Senones, and it is picked up later by *conati* and *insecuti,* while the main verbs are *expulerunt* and *non fuerunt.*

The hostility of the Senones was a serious matter for Caesar since they lay on the direct route from North Gaul to Provence and Italy.

6. **Cavarinum . . . interficere . . . conati.** See Introduction, p. 3. Here is another example of the appointment of a client king leaving rancour among his fellow-citizens.

16. **praeter Aeduos et Remos.** See Index of Proper Names. The Aedui had been allies of the Romans since 121 B.C., while the friendship of the Remi since 57 B.C. had greatly facilitated Caesar's conquest of Belgium.

21. **haud scio mirandumne sit.** Compare the colloquial English expression: 'I don't know that it is so very remarkable.'

22. **cum . . . tum . . .** See Vocabulary.

LV

8. **Ariovisti bello et Tencterorum transitu.** See Introduction, p. 11 and p. 13. This passage makes it clear that whether Caesar, in invading Germany, desired the conquest of part of the country or not, his incursion had at any rate had the effect of stopping German interference on the Gallic side of the Rhine.

LVI

1. **ultro ad se veniri,** an impersonal passive; translate 'that they were coming to him of their own accord.'

2. **conscientia facinoris,** the Senones because of the attempted assassination of Cavarinus (ch. LIV), the Carnutes because of the murder of Tasgetius (ch. XXV).

3. **Nervios Aduatucosque.** The Nervii and the Aduatuci were tough fighters, for in 57 B.C., according to Caesar's own account, they had been nearly wiped out; yet they lived to storm Cicero's camp. And even after the defeat described in ch. LI, they were still conspiring.

6. **quo,** adverbial; translate 'for to this council.'

11. **quem supra demonstravimus,** in ch. III.

LVII

1. **munitissimis castris sese teneret.** In ch. XXIV, we were told that Labienus' camp was among the Remi, on the frontier of the Treveri. He was, of course, meant to watch the latter people. The site of his camp has been placed at Mouzon.

7. **equitesque undique evocat.** See note on ch. XLVI, line 11.

13. **timorisque opinionem . . . augebat.** Caesar had employed the same stratagem against the Nervii (ch. L).

LVIII

2. **nocte una,** 'in the course of a single night,' *i.e.* the definite time which he had fixed for their assembly (ch. LVII, line 7). Indutiomarus' contempt for Labienus had evidently led his sentries to relax their vigilance.

11. **ubi visum est,** 'when they thought fit.'

13. **praecipit atque interdicit.** Understand *praecipit* with *unum omnes peterent* and *interdicit* with *neu quis quem prius vulneret,* but translate the two together: 'gave stringent orders' (Rice Holmes).

17. **mora reliquorum,** 'the delay caused by dealing with the others.'

20. **hominis.** In ch. VII, line 25, Caesar used this word to show ill-feeling: here he uses it to show admiration. We might use 'the man' or 'the fellow' in the same way.

26. **quietiorem Galliam.** Gaul was quieter, but it was not subdued. It had been too quickly overrun in the first place, and this revolt among the Belgae was the prelude to a widespread rebellion that made a second conquest necessary (Introduction, p. 17).

INDEX OF PROPER NAMES

(*N.B.* If a Roman has two or three names, you will find him by looking up his last name.)

Aduatuca, -ae (*f.*): site of the camp of Sabinus and Cotta in the winter of 54 B.C.; possibly at Tongres in Belgium.

Aduatuci, -orum (*m.*): a Belgic tribe living on the R. Meuse; conquered by Caesar in 57 B.C., rebelled in 54 B.C. and defeated.

Aedui, -orum (*m.*): a powerful Celtic tribe, traditional rivals of the Arverni for the supremacy in Central Gaul; 121 B.C., aided by the Romans and became their allies; 61 B.C., defeated by Ariovistus and the Germans; 58 B.C., appealed to Caesar for help against the Helvetii.

Africus, -i (*m.*): the south-west wind (so-called because it blows from Africa to Italy).

Ahenobarbus, Lucius Domitius: consul in 54 B.C.

Ambiorix, -igis (*m.*): joint king with Catuvolcus of the Eburones, and leader of the rising that annihilated the troops of Sabinus and Cotta.

Ancalites, -um (*m.*): a British tribe, mentioned only by Caesar.

Arduenna Silva: the forest of the Ardennes Mountains in south-east Belgium.

Aremoricae, -arum (*f. pl.*): a Celtic word meaning 'maritime.'

Ariovistus, -i (*m.*): leader of the Suebi, a German tribe that invaded Gaul in 71 B.C. on the invitation of the Sequani; received title of *amicus populi Romani* from the senate, 60 B.C.; driven from Gaul by Caesar, 58 B.C., and died shortly after.

Arpineius, Gaius: a Roman knight, serving with Sabinus.

Atrebas, -atis (*m.*): an Atrebatian, *i.e.* a member of the Belgic tribe of the Atrebates, whose continental capital was Nemetacum (Arras), and of whom a number settled in Britain with their capital at Silchester.

Atrius, Quintus: one of Caesar's officers, left in charge of the ships on the Kentish coast in 54 B.C.

Balventius, Titus: a centurion in Sabinus' army.

Belgae, -arum: a half-Celtic, half-German tribe that invaded Gaul from Germany in the 2nd century B.C., and invaded S.E. Britain in the 1st century B.C.

Belgium, -i (*n.*): a general name for the territory inhabited by the continental Belgic tribes, wider than modern Belgium.
Bellovaci, -orum (*m.*): a Belgic tribe living between the Seine and the Somme; surrendered to Caesar in 57 B.C., reconquered in 51 B.C., after the revolt of Vercingetorix.
Bibroci, -orum (*m.*): a British tribe, mentioned only by Caesar.
Britanni, -orum (*m.*): Britons.
Britannia, -ae (*f.*): Britain.

Caesar, Gaius Julius: born 102 or 101 B.C.; a democratic politician down to 63 B.C., then elected Pontifex Maximus (63 B.C.) and praetor (62 B.C.); 61 B.C., governor of Further (South) Spain; 59 B.C., consul; 58 B.C., governor of the Gallic provinces and Illyria; 49 B.C., civil war with Pompey; dictator. Defeated Pompey's sympathisers at Ilerda (49 B.C.), Pompey himself at Pharsalia (48 B.C.), and other republicans at Thapsus (46 B.C.) and Munda (45 B.C.); murdered 44 B.C.
Cantium, -i (*n.*): Kent.
Carnutes, -ium (*m.*): a Celtic tribe living between the Seine and the Loire; conquered by Caesar 57 B.C.; rebelled 53 B.C.; began the great rebellion.
Carvilius, -i (*m.*): one of the four kings of Kent.
Cassi, -orum (*m.*): a British tribe, mentioned only by Caesar.
Cassivellaunus, -i (*m.*): chief of one of the Belgic tribes in Britain, whose capital was in Hertfordshire (Wheathampstead).
Catuvolcus, -i (*m.*): joint-king with Ambiorix of the Eburones, and leader of the rising that annihilated the troops of Sabinus and Cotta; committed suicide, 53 B.C.
Caurus, -i (*m.*): north-west wind.
Cavarinus, -i (*m.*): king set over the Senones by Caesar; expelled 54 B.C.
Cenimagni, -orum (*m.*): a British tribe, mentioned only by Caesar.
Ceutrones, -um (*m.*): a *pagus* of the Nervii.
Cicero, Quintus: brother of the famous orator and one of Caesar's *legati* in Gaul.
Cingetorix, -igis (*m.*): (i) a chief of the Treveri, (ii) one of the four kings of Kent.
Commius, -i (*m.*): chief of the Atrebates, and influential on both sides of the Channel; 55–54 B.C., with Caesar in Britain; 53 B.C., kept watch for Caesar over the Menapii; 52 B.C., rebelled against Caesar and later surrendered; possibly to be identified with the Commius, who later ruled over the Atrebates in Britain.
Cotta, Lucius Aurunculeius: one of Caesar's *legati* in Gaul.
Crassus, Marcus Licinius: son of the famous financier of the same name, and one of Caesar's provincial quaestors in Gaul. Not to be confused with his younger brother, P.

Crassus, who conquered Aquitania in 56 B.C.

Dumnorix, -igis (*m.*): the most powerful chieftain of the Aedui and leader of the anti-Roman faction in that tribe; 58 B.C., in secret league with the Helvetii; 54 B.C., reluctant to go with Caesar to Britain and ran away, but was pursued and killed.

Durus, Quintus Laberius: a military tribune, killed in Britain in 54 B.C.

Eburones, -um (*m.*): a tribe of Germanic origin, living on the Gallic side of the Rhine.

Esubii, -orum (*m.*): a Celtic tribe, living in Normandy.

Fabius, Gaius: one of Caesar's *legati*.

Fortuna, -ae (*f.*): Fortune, thought of as a goddess.

Gallia, -ae (*f.*): one or other of the Gallic provinces, e.g. *Gallia Citerior*: Cisalpine Gaul, between the Alps and the River Po.

Galli, -orum (*m.*): Gauls.

Gallicus, -a, -um: Gallic.

Geidumni, -orum (*m.*): a *pagus* of the Nervii.

Germani, -orum (*m.*): Germans.

Germania, -ae (*f.*): a general name for that part of Central Europe which was bounded by the Rhine, the Danube, the North Sea, and the Baltic, including modern Germany but less definite.

Germanicus, -a, -um: German.

Grudii, -orum (*m.*): a *pagus* of the Nervii.

Hibernia, -ae, (*f.*): Ireland.

Hispania, -ae (*f.*): Spain.

Hispanus, -a, -um: Spanish.

Illyricum, -i (*n.*): a district east of the Adriatic, annexed by Rome in 167 B.C., and organised as a province about a century later.

Indutiomarus, -i (*m.*): a chief of the Treveri.

Itius Portus: the harbour on the north coast of France from which Caesar sailed to Britain, variously identified as Boulogne and Wissant (see note on ch. v, l. 1).

Iunius, Quintus: a follower of Caesar from Spain.

Labienus, Titus Attius: Caesar's ablest *legatus* in Gaul, who proved especially competent in dealing with the tribes near the Rhine; 54 B.C., was left in command of Gaul, while Caesar was in Britain; in the Civil War, deserted to Pompey and fought against Caesar; 45 B.C., killed at Munda.

Levaci, -orum (*m.*): a *pagus* of the Nervii.

Lucanius, Quintus: a centurion in Sabinus' army.

Lugotorix, -igis (*m.*): a British chieftain.

Mandubracius, -i (*m.*): son of the king of the Trinobantes. His father was killed by Cassivellaunus, and he himself fled to Caesar, and on Cassivellaunus' defeat was reinstated in his kingdom.

Meldi, -orum (*m.*): a Celtic tribe (modern Meaux), living between the Marne and the Seine, which supplied Caesar with 60 ships.

Menapii, -orum (*m.*): a Celtic tribe, living near the mouth of the Rhine on the Gallic side.

Mona, -ae (*f.*): Anglesea, though Caesar gives the name to the Isle of Man.

Morini, -orum (*m.*): a Belgic tribe on the coast between the Seine and the Schelde, in whose territory lay Caesar's port of departure for Britain; did not finally surrender till 55 B.C.

Moritasgus, -i (*m.*): brother of Cavarinus, and king of the Senones at the time of Caesar's conquest of this territory.

Mosa, -ae (*f.*): the River Meuse.

Nervii, -orum (*m.*): one of the most powerful of the Belgic tribes, living on the east bank of the River Schelde.

Oceanus, -i (*m.*): the Atlantic.

Padus, -i (*m.*): the River Po.

Petrosidius, Lucius: standard-bearer in Sabinus' army.

Pirustae, -arum (*m.*): an Illyrian tribe.

Plancus, Lucius Munatius: one of Caesar's *legati* in Gaul.

Pleumoxii, -orum (*m.*): a *pagus* of the Nervii.

Pompeius, Gnaius: a Gallic interpreter in Sabinus' army.

Pulcher, Appius Claudius: consul in 54 B.C.

Pullo, Titus: a centurion in Cicero's army.

Remi, -orum (*m.*): a Belgic tribe (modern Rheims), which surrendered to Caesar on his invasion of the Belgae in 57 B.C. and remained loyal to him throughout.

Rhenus, -i (*m.*): the River Rhine.

Roscius, Lucius: one of Caesar's officers in Gaul.

Rufus, Publius Sulpicius: one of Caesar's *legati* in Gaul.

Sabinus, Quintus Titurius: one of Caesar's *legati* in Gaul.

Samarobriva, -ae (*f.*): Amiens (lit. = the bridge on the Samara).

Segontiaci, -orum (*m.*): a British tribe, mentioned by Caesar, whose name is also found on coins.

Segovax, -acis (*m.*): one of the four kings of Kent.

Senones, -um: a Celtic tribe living between the Seine and the Yonne, whose capital was Agediucum (modern Sens); submitted to Caesar in 57 B.C., but rebelled in 54 B.C.; put down in 53 B.C., but rebelled again in 52 B.C. and finally subdued by Labienus.

Tamesis, -is (*m.*): the River Thames.

Tasgetius, -i (*m.*): appointed king of the Carnutes by Caesar.

Taximagulus, -i (*m.*): one of the four kings of Kent.

Tencteri, -orum (*m.*) **:** a German tribe that invaded Gaul in 55 B.C. and were virtually annihilated by Caesar as a result.

Trebonius, Gaius: one of Caesar's *legati* in Britain and Gaul; 55 B.C. tribune of the people; aided Caesar in Civil War, but was among those who murdered him in 44 B.C.

Treveri, -orum (*m.*) **:** a tribe of mixed German and Celtic origin (modern Trèves), living on either side of the Moselle.

Trinobantes, -um (*m.*) **:** a tribe living in east Herts and Essex, with their capital at Camulodunum (Colchester).

Veneticus, -a, -um: Venetian, pertaining to the Veneti, a Celtic tribe (modern Vannes) in south Britanny; *Veneticum bellum:* war with the Veneti.

Vertico, -onis (*m.*) **:** a Nervian nobleman in the camp of Cicero.

Volusenus, Gaius: a military tribune of high repute in Caesar's army.

Vorenus, Lucius: a centurion in Cicero's army.

VOCABULARY

(*N.B.* The quantity of vowels is marked only when the syllable is naturally long.)

ā, ab (*prep.* with *abl.*) **:** from, by, on the side of; **a millibus passuum octo:** at a distance of.

abdō, -ere, -didī, -ditum (*v.t.*) **:** to hide.

abdūcō, -ere, -xī, -ctum (*v.t.*) **:** to lead away, carry off.

abiciō, -ere, iēcī, -iectum (*v.t.*) **:** to throw away, lay down (arms).

abiēs, -etis (*f.*) **:** fir.

absistō, -ere, -stitī (*v.i.*) **:** to desist, keep aloof; **ab signis legionibusque absistere,** *i.e.* hesitate to attack.

absum, abesse, āfuī (*v.i.*) **:** to be absent or distant.

ac (*conj.*) **:** and (emphatic), and moreover.

accēdō, -ere, -cessī, -cessum (*v.i.*) **:** approach, move up; **huc accedit:** there is a further point (used as passive of **addo**).

accersō = *arcesso.*

accidō, -ere, -cidī (*v.i.*) **:** to happen.

accīdō, -ere, -cīdī, -cīsum (*v.t.*) **:** to cut into.

accipiō, -ere, -cēpī, -ceptum (*v.t.*) **:** to receive, learn.

accurātē, -ius, -issimē (*adv.*) **:** carefully, elaborately.

ācerrimē: see **ācriter.**

aciēs, -ēī (*f.*) **:** battle array (*i.e.* an army deployed for battle; *cf.* **agmen:** an army in line of march).

ācriter, ācrius, ācerrimē (*adv.*) **:** fiercely, vigorously.

actuārius, -a, -um: driven by oars.

acūtus, -a, -um: sharp.

ad (*prep.* with *acc.*) **:** to, towards, up to, by, near; for, for the purpose of; **ad nutum et ad tempus,** *i.e.* promptly at the word of command; **ad clamorem hominum:** at the men's shouts; **ad altitudinem valli** (ch. XLII) **:** in proportion to.

adactus: see **adigo.**

adaequō, -āre, -āvī, -ātum (*v.t.* and *i.*) **:** to make equal to, to equal, rival.

addō, -ere, -didī, -ditum (*v.t.*) **:** to add.

adducō, -ere, -duxī, -ductum (*v.t.*) **:** to lead to, bring to, induce.

ademptus: see **adimo.**

adeō, -īre, -iī ,-itum (*v.i.*) **:** go to, approach, visit.

adeo (*adv.*) **:** so, to such a degree, in fact.

adferō, -ferre, -tulī, -latum (*v.t.*) **:** to bring, cause, allege.

adficiō, -ere, -fēcī, -fectum (*v.t.*) **:** to affect, influence, treat.

adflictō, -āre, -āvī, -ātum (*v.t.*): to damage, wreck.

adfligō, -ere, -flixī, -flictum (*v.t.*): to knock down, damage.

adgregō, -āre, -āvī, -ātum (*v.t.* with **se**): gather round, join.

adhaerescō, -ere, -haesī, -haesum (*v.i.*): to cling to, stick to.

adhibeō, -ēre, -uī, -itum (*v.t.*): to summon, call in.

adhortor, -ārī, -ātus sum (*v.t.*): to encourage, urge on.

adiciō, -ere, -iēcī, -iectum (*v.t.*): to throw up against.

adigō, -ere, -ēgī, -actum (*v.t.*): to push up, drive towards, drive home (a weapon).

adimō, -ere, -ēmī, -emptum (*v.t.*): to take away.

adipiscor, -ī, adeptus sum (*v.t.*): to win, obtain.

aditus, -ūs (*m.*): approach, access, right of approach.

adiungō, -ere, -nxī, -nctum (*v.t.*): to unite, annex, win over.

adiutor, -ōris (*m.*): helper.

adiūvō, -āre, -iūvī, -iūtum (*v.t.*): to help.

adliciō, -ere, -lexī, -lectum (*v.t.*): to entice, induce.

administrō, -āre, -āvī, -ātum (*v.t.*): to manage, carry out.

admīror, -ārī, -ātus sum (*v.t.*): to wonder at, admire, feel surprised.

admittō, -ere, -mīsī, -missum (*v.t.*): to let go, commit (a crime), incur (disgrace).

admodum (*adv.*): very, quite, greatly, about (with numerals).

admoneō, -ēre, -uī, -itum (*v.t.*): to warn.

adolescō, -ere, -olēvī, adultum (*v.i.*): to grow up; **adolescens**: a youth.

adorior, -orīrī, -ortus sum (*v.t.*): to attack.

adpellō, -ere, -pulī, -pulsum (*v.t.*): to drive to, bring (a ship) to land.

adplicō, -āre, -āvī, -ātum (*v.a.*): to lean against, put against.

adportō, -āre, -āvī, -ātum (*v.t.*): to carry, to convey.

adpropinquō, -āre, -āvī, -ātum (*v.i.*): to approach, draw near.

adsistō, -ere, -stitī (*v.i.*): to stand by.

adsuēfaciō, -ere, -fēcī, -factum (*v.t.*): to accustom; passive =get used (to anything).

adsuescō, -ere, -ēvī, -ētum (*v.i.*): to grow accustomed.

adsum, -esse, -fuī (*v.i.*): to be at hand, stand by.

adventus, -ūs (*m.*): approach.

adversus, -a, -um: opposite, facing, unfavourable.

advertō, -ere, -ī, -sum (*v.t.*): to turn towards; **animum advertere**: to notice.

advolō, -āre, -āvī, -ātum (*v.i.*): to rush at, with **ad**: to swoop down upon.

aedificium, -ī (*n.*): a building.

aedificō, -āre, -āvī, -ātum (*v.t.*): to build.

aeger, -ra, -grum: ill, sick.

aegrē, -rius, aegerrimē (*adv.*): with difficulty.

aequinoctium, -ī (*n.*): equinox, season of the year (mid-spring and mid-autumn) when day and night are equal.

aequitās, -ātis (*f.*): fairness; **animi aequitas**: contentment.

aequō, -āre, -āvī, -ātum (*v.t.*) **:** to make equal.

aequus, -a, -um : equal, level, advantageous; **aequo animo :** calmly.

aes, aeris (*n.*) **:** copper, bronze.

aestās, -ātis (*f.*) **:** summer.

aestimātiō, -ōnis (*f.*) **:** valuation.

aestimō, -āre, -āvī, -ātum (*v.t.*) **:** weigh, value; **litem aestimare :** to assess the amount of damage

aestus, -ūs (*m.*) **:** tide, current, heat.

aetās, -ātis (*f.*) **:** age.

Āfricus, (*sc.* **ventus**), **-ī** (*m.*) **:** south-west wind.

ager, -grī (*m.*) **:** land, territory (*often in pl.*).

agger, -eris (*m.*) **:** rampart, embankment, material; **aggerem adicere :** to pile earth.

agmen, -inis (*n.*) **:** column, an army on the march in column; **primum agmen :** the van; **novissimum agmen :** the rear.

agō, -ere, ēgī, actum (*v.t.*) **:** to do, drive; **agere de :** to treat about, discuss.

agricultūra, -ae (*f.*) **:** farming, husbandry.

alacer, -cris, -cre : keen, eager.

alacritās, -ātis (*f.*) **:** keenness, enthusiasm, dash.

albus, -a, -um : white; **album plumbum :** tin.

aliās (*adv.*) **:** at another time; **alias . . . alias . . . :** at one time . . . at another time.

aliēnus, -a, -um : belonging to another, foreign, unfavourable.

aliō (*adv.*) **:** to another place.

aliquamdiū (*adv.*) **:** for a considerable time.

aliquantus, -a, -um : considerable; **aliquantum** (*neut.*, used as *subst.*, often with *gen.*) **:** a considerable part.

aliquī, -qua, -quod : some.

aliquis, -quis, -quid (*indef. pron.*) **:** some one, something.

aliter (*adv.*) **:** otherwise, in a different way; **aliter ac :** differently from, otherise than.

alius, -a, -ud : other, different; **alios alii . . . exciperent :** they relieved each other.

alō, -ere, aluī, altum (*v.t.*) **:** to feed, foster, support.

alter, -era, -um (in ch. XXVII *dat. sing.* **alterae**) **:** the one or the other of two; the latter (ch. III); **alteri . . . alteri :** one party . . . the other party.

altitūdō, -inis (*f.*) **:** height, depth.

altus, -a, -um : high, deep; (*subst.*) **altum :** open sea, deep water.

āmentia, -iae (*f.*) **:** madness.

amīcitia, -iae (*f.*) **:** friendship.

amīcus, -a, -um : friendly, well-disposed.

āmittō, -ere, -mīsī, -missum (*v.t.*) **:** to lose.

ammentum, -ī (*n.*) **:** thong, strap.

amplificō, -āre, -āvī, -atum (*v.t.*) **:** to widen, increase.

amplitūdō, -inis (*f.*) **:** width, power.

amplius (*compar. adv., absol.* or with *abl.*) **:** more than, farther.

amplus, -a, -um : considerable, large.

an (*conj.*) **:** or.

ancora, -ae (*f.*) **:** anchor; **in ancoris exspectāre :** to wait at anchor; **ad ancoras deligatae :** riding at anchor.

angulus, -ī (*m.*) : corner, extreme point.
angustiae, -ārum (*f.*) : defile, narrowness; **angustiis viarum** : by making the streets narrow.
angustus, -a, -um : narrow, contracted; **angustius milites collocāre** : to pack rather tightly; **frumentum angustius provenerat** : *i.e.* rather scantily.
anima, -ae (*f.*) : soul.
animadvertō, -ere, -tī, -sum (*v.t.*) : perceive, notice.
animal, -ālis (*n.*) : animal.
animus, -ī (*m.*) : mind, intention, feelings, courage; **animi causa** : for pastime.
annōtinus, -a, -um : last year's, a year old.
annus, -ī (*m.*) : year.
anser, -eris (*m.*) : goose.
ante (*prep.* with *acc.* and *adv.*) : before.
antecedō, -ere, -cessī, -cessum (*v.t.* and *i.*) : to precede, go before, excel.
antecursor, -ōris (*m.*) : forerunner; (*pl.*) advanced guard.
anteferō, -ferre, -tuli, -lātūm (*v.t.*) : to prefer.
antepōnō, -ere, -posuī, -positum (*v.t.*) : prefer.
antiquitus (*adv.*) : in times past, at a distant period.
aperiō, -īre, aperuī, apertum (*v.t.*) : to open, disclose; **apertus** : open, exposed.
App. : Appius (Roman *praenomen*).
appellō, -āre, -āvī, -ātum (*v.t.*) : to call, name, call upon.
aptus, -a, -um : fit.
apud (*prep.* with *acc.*) : at, near, among, with.
aqua, -ae (*f.*) : water.
aquila, -ae (*f.*) : eagle, the standard of a legion (see Intro., p. 23, and Pl. IX).
aquilifer, -erī (*m.*) : standard-bearer.
arbiter, -trī (*m.*) : umpire.
arbitror, -ārī, -ātus sum (*v.i.*) : consider, believe.
arbor, -oris (*f.*) : tree.
arbitrium, -iī (*n.*) : decision, judgment.
arcessō, -ere, -īvī, -ītum (*v.t.*) : to summon.
argentum, -ī (*n.*) : silver.
argilla, -ae (*f.*) : clay.
āridus, -a, -um : dry; (*subst.*) **aridum** : the dry land.
arma, -ōrum (*n. pl.*) : arms, weapons.
armō, -āre, -āvī, -ātum (*v.t.*) : to arm, fit out.
arripiō, -ere, -ripuī, -reptum (*v.t.*) : to seize.
ars, -tis (*f.*) : art, skill.
articulus, -ī (*m.*) : joint.
artificium, -iī (*m.*) : skilled labour, handicraft.
ascendō, -ere, -scendī, -scensum (*v.t.*) : ascend, climb.
ascensus, -ūs (*m.*) : ascent, way up.
asper, -era, -erum (*adj.*) : rough, violent.
attexō, -ere, -texuī, -textum (*v.t.*) : to weave on, fasten to.
aspectus, -ūs (*m.*) : sight, appearance.
at (*conj.*) : but, yet.
atque, āc (*conj.*) and (emphatic); **simul atque** : as soon as; **aliter ac** : differently from.
attingō, -ere, -tigī, -tactum (*v.t.*) : to adjoin, extend to, reach.
attribuō, -ere, -uī, -ūtum (*v.t.*) : to assign.

auctor, -ōris (*m.*): adviser, supporter; **profectionis auctor**: one who approves of setting out.
auctoritās, -ātis (*f.*): influence, authority, prestige.
audacter, audacius, audacissimē (*adv.*): boldly.
audax, -ācis (*adj.*): bold, daring.
audeō, -ēre, ausus sum (*v.t.* and *i.*): to dare, venture.
audiō, -īre, -īvī, -ītum (*v.t.*): to hear; **dicto audiens**: obedient.
augeō, -ēre, auxī, auctum (*v.t.*): to increase.
aureus, -a, -um: golden.
aut (*conj.*): or; **aut . . . aut . . .**: either . . . or.
autem (*conj.*): but, now, moreover.
autumnus, -ī (*m.*): autumn.
auxilior, -ārī, -ātus sum (*v.i.*): to bring help.
auxilium, -ī (*n.*): help; (*pl.*) auxiliaries, reinforcements.
āvertō, -ere, -tī, -sum (*v.t.*): to turn away.

balteus, -ī (*m.*): sword-belt.
barbarus, -a, -um: uncivilised, foreign; *subst.* **barbarus**: native, foreigner, barbarian.
bellum, -ī (*n.*): war.
bene, melius, optimē (*adv.*): well.
beneficium, -ī (*n.*): kindness, favour.
benevolentia, -ae (*f.*): goodwill, kindness.
bīduum, -ī (*n.*): a space of two days.
bipertīto (*adv.*): in two divisions.
bīs (*adv.*): twice.
bonus, -a, -um (*adj.*): good; *neut. pl.* = property.
bōs, bovis (*c.*): ox, cow.
brevis, -e: short; **brevi**: in a short space, in a moment.
brūma, -ae (*f.*): the shortest day, winter; **sub bruma**: about the winter solstice, *i.e.* December 21.

C: Gaius (Roman *praenomen*); 100.
cadō, -ere, cecidī, cāsum (*v.i.*): to fall, be killed.
caedes, -is (*f.*): slaughter, massacre.
caelestis, e (*adj.*): heavenly, celestial; *pl.* the gods.
caespēs, -itis (*m.*): a sod.
caeruleus, -a, -um: dark-coloured, bluish.
calamitās, -ātis (*f.*): disaster, injury.
campus, -ī (*m.*): plain.
capillus, -ī (*m.*): hair.
capiō, -ere, cēpī, captum (*v.t.*): to take, capture; **consilium capere**: to form a plan; **insulam, portus capere**: to reach, 'make.'
captīvus, -ī (*m.*): prisoner.
caput, -itis (*n.*)): head.
caro, carnis (*f.*): flesh.
carus, -a, -um (*adj.*): dear, valued.
casa, -ae (*f.*): hut.
castellum, -ī (*n.*): fort, fortified post.
castra, -ōrum (*n. pl.*): camp.
cāsus, -ūs (*m.*): chance, accident, emergency.
Caurus, -ī (*m.*): north-west wind.
causa, -ae (*f.*): cause, reason; **causā**, (preceded by *gen.*): for the sake of.
cēdō, -ere, cessī, cessum (*v.i.*): to yield, retreat.

celer, -eris, -ere: swift.
celeritās, -ātis (*f.*): speed.
celeriter, celerius, celerrimē (*adv.*): quickly.
centum: hundred.
centuriō, -iōnis (*m.*): centurion.
cernō, -ere, crēvī, crētum (*v.t.*): to see, discern.
certāmen, -inis (*n.*): struggle, rivalry.
certē (*adv.*): certainly, at any rate.
certus, -a, -um: sure, accurate. certain; **certiorem facere:** to inform.
cēterī, -ae, -a: the rest, all other.
cingō, -ere, -nxī, -nctum (*v.t.*): to surround.
circiter (*prep.* with *acc.*): about.
circuitus, -ūs (*m.*): circuit, compass, circumference.
circum (*prep.* with *acc.*): about, around, near.
circumdō, -are, -dedī, -datum (*v.t.*): to surround, place round.
circumeō, -īre, -iī, -itum (*v.t.*): to go round, inspect.
circumsistō, -ere, -stetī (*v.t.*): to surround, rally round.
circumspiciō, -ere, -spexī, -spectum (*v.t.*): to examine, look round at.
circumveniō, -īre, -vēnī, -ventum (*v.t.*): to surround, overreach.
citerior, -ius (*comp. adj.*): on this side, nearer.
citissimē (*adv., superl.* of **cito**): very quickly, very nimbly.
citrā (*prep.* with *acc.*): on this side of.
cīvitās, -ātis (*f.*): community, tribe.
clam (*adv.*): secretly.
clāmitō, -āre, -āvī, -ātum (*v.i.*): call repeatedly, insist loudly.
clāmor, -ōris (*m.*): shouting, uproar.
clārus, -a, -um: (*adj.*): renowned, loud, clear.
classis, -is (*f.*): fleet.
cliens, -tis (*m.*): retainer, dependant.
coactus, -ūs (*m.*): compulsion.
coeo, -īre, -iī, -itum (*v.i.*): to come together, assemble.
coerceō, -ēre, -uī, -itum (*v.t.*): to control, compel.
cōgitō, -āre, -āvī, -ātum (*v.t.*): to ponder, reflect upon.
cognoscō, -ere, cognōvī, cognitum, to get to know, discover.
cōgō, -ere, coēgī, coactum (*v.t.*): to compel, collect, concentrate.
cohors, -rtis (*f.*): cohort.
cohortor, -ārī, -ātūs sum (*v.t.*): to harangue, encourage, urge.
coiciō, -ere, coniēcī, coniectum (*v.t.*): to throw, hurl.
collaudō, -āre, -āvī, -ātum (*v.t.*): to praise highly.
colligō, -ere, collēgī, collectum (*v.t.*): to collect, rally.
collis, -is (*m.*): hill.
colō, -ere, -uī, cultum (*v.t.*): to cultivate.
color, -ōris (*m.*): colour.
commeātus, -ūs (*m.*): passage, provisions.
commemorō, -āre, -āvī, -ātum (*v.t.*): to recount, mention.
comminus (*adv.*): hand to hand, at close quarters.
committō, -ere, -mīsī, -missum (*v.t.*): to entrust, commit; **proelium committere:** to begin an action.
commodum, -ī (*n.*): advantage, profit.

commodus, -a, -um: advantageous, convenient; **commode:** adequately, conveniently.

commoror, -ārī, -ātus sum (*v.i.*): to stay, wait, delay.

commūniō, -īre, -īvī, -ītum (*v.t.*): to fortify strongly.

commūnis, -e: common, general, national.

commūtatiō, -ōnis (*f.*): change.

comparō, -āre, -āvī, -ātum (*v.t.*): to prepare, compare.

compellō, -ere, -pulī, -pulsum (*v.t.*): to drive together.

comperiō, -īre, -perī, -pertum (*v.t.*): to ascertain, detect.

compleō, -ēre, -ēvī, -ētum (*v.t.*): to fill, to man.

complūrēs, -ium: several.

comportō, -āre, -āvī, -ātum (*v.t.*): to bring together, collect.

comprehendō, -ere, -dī, -sum (*v.t.*): to seize, arrest.

comprobō, -āre, -āvī, -atum (*v.t.*): to confirm, justify.

concidō, -ere, -cidī (*v.i.*): to fall down, drop.

conciliō, -āre, -āvī, -ātum (*v.t.*): to procure, win over.

concilium, -ī (*n.*): meeting, assembly. Distinguish **concilium,** an assembly called together to hear a proclamation, and **consilium,** a council for consultation.

concitō, -āre, -āvī, -ātum (*v.t.*): to rouse, stir up.

conclāmō, -āre, -āvī, -ātum (*v.i.*): to rouse a cry, shout out together.

concurrō, -ere, -currī, -cursum (*v.i.*): to run together, rush.

concursō, -āre, -āvī, -ātum (*v.i.*): to rush about, rush from place to place.

concursus, -ūs (*m.*): thronging, collision.

condiciō, -ōnis (*f.*): condition, terms.

condūcō, -ere, -xī, -ctum (*v.t.*): to bring together, concentrate, hire.

conferō, -ferre, contulī, conlātum (*v.t.*): to bring together.

confertus, -a, -um (*perf. part.* of **confercio**): crowded together, close-packed.

confestim (*adv.*): immediately.

conficiō, -ere, -fēcī, -fectum (*v.t.*): to complete, accomplish; **confectus:** exhausted.

confīdō, -ere, -fīsus sum (*v.i.*, with *dat.* or *abl.*): to trust, rely on.

confīnium, -ī (*n.*): frontier.

confirmō, -āre, -āvī, -ātum (*v.t.*): to keep steady, reassure, affirm.

confiteor, -ērī, -fessus sum (*v.t.*): to acknowledge, admit.

conflagrō, -āre, -āvī, -ātum (*v.i.*): to burn, be on fire.

conflīgō, -ere, -flixī, -flictum (*v.i.*): to fight, engage with.

congredior, -ī, -gressus sum (*v.i.*): to engage, fight, meet.

coniunctim (*adv.*): jointly.

coniungō, -ere, -iunxī, -iunctum (*v.t.*): to join, unite.

coniūrātiō, -ōnis (*f.*): conspiracy.

conlocō, -āre, -āvī, -ātum (*v.t.*): to place, post, station.

conloquor, -ī, -locūtus sum (*v.i.*): to converse, hold a conference.

cōnor, -ārī, -ātus sum (*v.i.*): to attempt.

conquīrō, -ere, -quīsīvī, -quīsītum (*v.t.*) **:** to search for.

conscendō, -ere, -ndī, -nsum (*v.t.*) **:** to climb, mount, embark.

conscientia, -ae (*f.*) **:** consciousness, complicity.

conscrībō, -ere, -psī, -ptum (*v.t.*) **:** to write, enrol, raise (troops).

consector, -ārī, -ātus sum (*v.t.*) **:** to pursue, chase.

consentiō, -īre, -sī, -sum (*v.i.*) **:** to agree, make common cause.

consequor, -ī, -secūtus sum (*v.t.* and *i.*) **:** to pursue, follow, ensue.

consīdō, -ere, -sēdī, -sessum (*v.i.*) **:** to encamp, take up a position.

consilium, -ī (*n.*) **:** plan, council of war, meeting.

consimilis, -e : like.

consistō, -ere, -stitī, -stitum (*v.i.*) **:** to stand, keep one's position; **in orbem consistere :** to form a hollow square.

consōlōr, -ārī, -ātus sum (*v.t.*) **:** to reassure, cheer.

conspectus, -us (*m.*) **:** view, sight.

conspiciō, -spicere, -spexī, -spectum (*v.t.*) **:** to catch sight of, see.

conspicor, -ārī, -ātus sum (*v.t.*) **:** to observe, notice.

constipō, -āre, -āvī, -ātum (*v.t.*) **:** to crowd together.

constituō, -ere, -uī, -ūtum (*v.t.*) **:** to draw up, appoint, fix, resolve.

constō, -āre, -stiti (*v.i.*) **:** to be established; **constat :** it is agreed.

consuescō, -ere, -suēvī, -suētum (*v.i.*) **:** to grow accustomed; (*perf.*) be wont.

consuētūdō, -inis (*f.*) **:** custom.

consul, -ulis (*m.*) **:** consul; **L. Domitio, Ap. Claudio consulibus :** in the consulship of . . .

consulō, -ere, -suluī, -sultum (*v.i.*, with *dat.*) **:** to act in the interests of.

consultō (*adv.*) **:** on purpose.

consultō, -āre, -āvī, -ātum (*v.i.*) **:** to consult.

consūmō, -ere, -sumpsī, -sumptum (*v.t.*) **:** to spend (time), use up, waste.

consurgō, -ere, -surrexī, -surrectum (*v.i.*) **:** to stand up; **consurgitur ex consilio :** the council broke up.

contabulō, -āre, -āvī, -ātum (*v.t.*) **:** to furnish with platforms.

contāgiō, -ōnis (*f.*) **:** contact, contamination.

contemnō, -ere, -tempsi, -temptum (*v.t.*) **:** to despise.

contemptiō, -ōnis (*f.*) **:** contempt.

contendō, -ere, -dī, -tum (*v.i.*) **:** to hasten, push on, fight.

contentiō, -ōnis (*f.*) **:** rivalry.

contestor, -ārī, -ātus sum (*v.t.*) **:** to call to witness.

continens, -entis (*pres. part.* of **contineo**) **:** unbroken; (as *noun*) the mainland.

contineō, -ēre, -uī, -tentum (*v.t.*) **:** to bound limit, wall in, to restrain; **se continere :** to stand one's ground, remain.

contingō, -ere, -tigī, -tactum (*v.t.*) **:** to touch, reach.

continuus, -a, -um : successive, consecutive.

contiō, -ōnis (*f.*) **:** an assembly, speech.

contrā (*prep.* with *acc.* and *adv.*) : against, contrary to.
contrahō, -ere, -traxī, -tractum (*v.t.*) : to draw together, concentrate, reduce in size.
contrōversia, -ae (*f,*) : dispute.
contumēlia, -ae (*f.*) : affront, insult.
convallis, -is (*f.*) : valley.
conveniō, -īre, -vēnī, -ventum (*v.i.*) : to assemble, meet.
conventus, -ūs (*m.*) : meeting, assizes.
convertō, -ere, -tī, -sum (*v.t.*) : to change, turn, direct.
convocō, -āre, -āvī, -ātum (*v.a.*) : to call together.
co-orior, -īrī, -ortus sum (*v.i.*) : to arise, break out.
cōpia, -iae (*f.*) : plenty, abundance; (in *pl.*) forces, wealth.
cor, cordis (*n.*) : the heart.
cōram (*adv.*) : personally.
cornū, -ūs (*n.*) : wing, horn, flank.
corpus, -oris (*n.*) : body.
cotīdianus, -a, -um : daily.
cotīdiē (*adv.*) : daily, every day.
crātis, -is (*f.*) : fascine, wickerwork.
crēber, -bra, -brum : frequently close together.
crēdō, -ere, -didī, -ditum (*v.t.*) : to believe.
cruciātus, -ūs (*m.*) : torture.
culpa, -ae (*f.*) : blame, fault.
cultus, -ūs (*m.*) : mode of living.
cum (1) (*conj.*) : when, since, although; **cum . . . tum . . . .** : both . . . and . . .; (2) (*prep.* with *abl.*) with.
cupidē, -ius, -issimē (*adv.*) : eagerly.
cupiditās, -ātis (*f.*) : desire, eagerness, greed.
cupidus, -a, -um : fond of, eager for.
cūrō, -āre, -āvī, -ātum (*v.t.* with *acc.* and *gerund.*) : to see to, cause to be done.
currus, -ūs (*m.*) : chariot.
cursus, -ūs (*m.*) : speed, course; **cursum adaequare** : to keep pace with; **cursum tenere** : to keep one's course.
custōdia, -ae (*f.*) : guard, watch.

D : 500.
dē (*prep.* with *abl.*) : down from, concerning, about; **de improviso** : unexpectedly.
dēbeō, -ēre, -uī, -itum (*v.t.*) : to owe, be bound, ought.
dēcēdō, -ere, -cessī, -cessum (*v.i.*) : to depart, retire.
decem : ten.
dēcernō, -ere, -crēvī, -crētum (*v.t.*) : to decide, decree.
decimus, -a, -um : tenth.
dēclīvis, -e : sloping down.
dēcrētum, -ī (*n.*) : decree, decision.
dēdecus, -oris (*n.*) : disgrace.
dēditiō, -ōnis (*f.*) : surrender.
dēdō, -ere, dēdidī, dēditum (*v.t.*) : to give up, surrender.
dēdūcō, -ere, -duxī, -ductum (*v.t.*) : to launch, conduct, marry (a wife).
dēfatīgō, -āre, -āvī, -ātum (*v.t.*) : to wear out, exhaust.
dēfectiō, -ōnis (*f.*) : revolt.
dēfendō, -ere, -dī, -sum (*v.t.*): to defend, protect.
dēfensor, -ōris (*m.*) : defender.
dēferō, -ferre, -tulī, -lātum (*v.t.*) : to carry down, to report.
dēficiō, -ere, -fēcī, -fectum (*v.i.*) : to fail, be wanting, revolt.

dēfīgō, -ere, -fixī, -fixum (*v.t.*) : to fix down.

dēfugiō, -ere, -fūgī (*v.t.*) : to shun, avoid.

dēiciō, -ere, -iēcī, -iectum (*v.t.*) : to throw down, sweep down; **opinione deiectus** (ch. XLVIII) : disappointed in his expectation.

deinceps (*adv.*) : in succession.

deinde (*adv.*) : secondly, next, then.

dēligō, -āre, -āvī, -ātum (*v.t.*) : to tie, moor; **deligari ad ancoras** : to ride at anchor.

dēligō, -ere, -lēgī, -lectum (*v.t.*) : to choose, pick out.

dēmigrō, -āre, -āvī, -ātum (*v.t.*) : to leave one's post, retire from the fight.

dēmittō, -ere, -mīsī, -missum (*v.t.*) : to let down; **se demittere** : to descend.

dēmō, -ere, dempsī, demptum (*v.t.*) : to take down, take off.

dēmonstrō, -āre, -āvī, -ātum (*v.t.*) : to point out, mention, explain.

dēmum (*adv.*) : at last.

dēnī, -ae, -a : ten each, ten.

dēnique (*adv.*) : at length, finally.

densus, -a, -um : thick, crowded, close.

dēnuntiō, -āre, -āvī, -ātum (*v.t.*) : to warn, declare.

dēpellō, -ere, -pulī, -pulsum (*v.t.*) : to drive, drive away.

dēperdō, -ere, -didī, -ditum (*v.t.*) : to lose.

dēpereō, -īre, -iī (*v.i.*) : to perish.

dēpono, -ere, -posuī, -positum (*v.t.*) : to lay down. lose.

dēprecor, -ārī, -ātus sum (*v.t.* and *i.*) : to beg earnestly, sue for mercy.

dēprehendō, -ere, -dī, -sum (*v.t.*) : to catch, seize.

dērogō, -āre, -āvī, -ātum (*v.t.*) : to take away, withdraw.

dēscendō, -ere, -dī, -sum (*v.i.*) : to come down, descend, have recourse to.

dēserō, -ere, -seruī, -sertum (*v.t.*) : to leave, desert; **desertus** : lonely.

dēsertor, -ōris (*m.*) : runaway, deserter.

dēsīderō, -āre, -āvī, -ātum (*v.t.*) : to miss, long for, want.

dēsiliō, -īre, -siluī, -sultum (*v.i.*) : to jump down.

dēsistō, -ere, -stitī, -stitum (*v.i.*) : to cease.

dēspērātiō, -onis (*f.*) : despair.

dēspērō, -āre, -āvī, -ātum (*v.t.* and *i*) : to despair, despair of.

dēsum, -esse, -fuī (*v.i.*) : to be wanting; (with *dat.*) to fail, desert.

dēterreō, -ere, -uī, -itum (*v.t.*) : to frighten, deter.

dētrīmentum, -ī (*n.*) : loss, damage.

dēturbō, -āre, -āvī, -ātum (*v.t.*) : to throw down, drive off, send flying.

deus, -ī (*m.*) : god.

dēvehō, -ere, -vexī, -vectum (*v.t.*) : to bring.

dēvoveō, -ere, -vōvī, -vōtum (*v.t.*) : to devote, dedicate.

dexter, -tra, -trum (-tera, -terum) (*adj.*) : right, on the right hand.

dīcō, -ere, -xī, -ctum (*v.t.*) : to say, mention, name.

dictum, -ī (*n.*): word, command.

diēs, -ēī (*pl. m.*) : day, season.

differō, -ferre, distulī, dīlātum (*v.t.*) : to postpone, delay; (*v.i.*) to differ.

difficultās, -ātis (*f.*) **:** difficulty.

diffīdō, -ere, -fisus sum (*v.i.*) **:** to distrust, feel anxious for.

diffundō, -ere, -fūdī, -fūsum (*v.t.*) **:** to spread out.

dignitās, -ātis (*f.*) **:** dignity, rank, distinction.

diūdicō, -āre, -āvī, -ātum (*v.t.*) **:** to decide.

dīligenter (*adv.*) **:** carefully, attentively; **parum diligenter,** carelessly.

dīligentia, -ae (*f.*) **:** vigilance, care.

dīligō, -ere, -lēxī, lectum (*v.t.*) **:** to love.

dīmicō, -āre, -āvī, -ātum (*v.i.*) **:** to fight.

dīmidium, -ī (*n.*) **:** a half.

dīmittō, -ere, -mīsī, -missum (*v.t.*) **:** to dismiss, send about.

discēdō, -ere, -cessī, -cessum (*v.i.*) **:** to withdraw, depart.

discessus, -ūs (*m.*) **:** departure, retreat.

discō, -ere, didicī (*v.t.*) **:** to learn.

dispār, -paris (*adj.*) **:** unequal.

dispergō, -ere, -spersī, -spersum (*v.t.*) **:** to scatter.

dispōnō, -ere, -posuī, -positum (*v.t.*) **:** to arrange, place at intervals, post.

disputātiō, -ōnis (*f.*) **:** argument.

dissensiō, -ōnis (*f.*) **:** conflict, quarrelling.

dissentiō, -īre, -sī, -sum (*v.i.*) **:** to differ in opinion, disagree.

distribuō, -ere, -buī, -būtum (*v.t.*) **:** to distribute, assign.

diū, diūtius, diutissimē (*adv.*) **:** for a long time; (*comp.*) too long.

diūtinus, -a, -um (*adj.*) **:** lasting, long.

dīversus, -a, -um (*adj.*) **:** separated, remote.

dīvidō, -ere, -vīsī, -vīsum (*v.t.*) **:** to divide, separate.

do, dare, dedī, datum (*v.t.*) **:** to give; **in fugam dare:** to put to flight; **arbitros dare:** to appoint umpires.

doceō, -ēre, -uī, doctum (*v.t.*) **:** to teach, explain, inform.

doleō, -ēre, -uī, -itum (*v.i.*) **:** grieve, feel resentment.

dolor, -ōris (*m.*) **:** grief, grievance, indignation.

domesticus, -a, -um: internal, at home; **domesticum bellum:** war at home, civil war.

dominus, -ī (*m.*) **:** master, owner

domus, -ūs (*f.*) **:** house, home; **domi:** at home; **domo:** from home; **domum:** homewards.

dubitatiō, -onis (*f.*) **:** doubt, hesitation.

ducentī, -ae, -a: 200.

dūcō, -ere, duxī, ductum (*v.t.*) **:** to lead, consider.

dum (*conj.*) **:** while, until.

duo, -ae, -o: two.

duodecim: twelve.

duodēnī, -ae, -a: twelve each, twelve.

dūplicō, -āre, -āvī, -ātum (*v.t.*) **:** to double.

dūrō, -āre, -āvī, -ātum (*v.t.*) **:** to harden.

dūrus, -a, -um (*adj.*) **:** hard, difficult; **si quid durius . . . :** if any disaster, anything untoward . . .

dux, ducis (*c.*) **:** leader, general, chieftain, guide.

ē, ex (*prep.* with *abl.*) **:** out of, from; **ex consuetudine:** according to custom; **una ex parte:** on one side.

eā (*adv.*) **:** by that way.
ēdūcō, -ere, -duxī, -ductum (*v.t.*) **:** to lead out.
efferō, -ferre, extūlī, ēlātūm (*v.t.*) **:** to bring out, carry, publish, spread (news).
efficiō, -ere, -fēcī, -fectum (*v.t.*) **:** to bring about, accomplish; **tantum efficiunt:** they become so efficient.
effugiō, -ere, -fūgī, -fugitum (*v.i.*) **:** to escape.
ego: I.
ēgredior, -gredī, -gressus sum (*v.i.*) **:** to go out, disembark.
ēgregius, -a, -um: exceptional, eminent; **egregie** (*adv.*) **:** exceedingly, admirably.
ēgressus, -ūs (*m.*) **:** going out, landing, landing-place.
ēiciō, -ere, ēiēcī, ēiectum (*v.t.*) **:** to cast out; **se eicere:** to rush out; **eicere in litus:** to drive ashore.
ēlābor, -ī, elapsus sum (*v.i.*) **:** to escape, slip away.
ēmittō, -ere, -mīsī, -missum (*v.t.*) **:** to send out.
enim (*conj.*) for.
ēnuntiō, -āre, -āvī, -ātum (*v.t.*) **:** to disclose, tell.
eō (*adv.*) **:** to that place; **eo magis:** all the more; **eo . . . quod:** on this account . . . that . . .
eō, īre, īvī or **iī, itum** (*v.i.*) **:** to go.
eōdem (*adv.*) **:** to the same place, in the same direction.
epistula, -ae (*f.*) **:** letter, dispatch.
eques, -itis (*m.*) **:** horseman; (*pl.*) cavalry.
equester, -tris, -tre: on horseback; **equestre proelium:** cavalry fight.
equitātus, -ūs (*m.*) **:** cavalry.
equus, -ī (*m.*) **:** horse.
ergā (*prep.* with *acc.*) **:** towards.
ērigō, -ere, -rexī, -rectum (*v.t.*) **:** to raise, set up.
ēruptiō, -ōnis (*f.*) **:** sortie.
essedārius, -ī (*m.*) **:** charioteer.
essedum, -ī (*m.*) **:** chariot.
et (*conj.*) **:** and; **et . . . et . . .:** both . . . and . . .
etiam (*conj.*) **:** also, too, even.
etsī (*conj.*) **:** although, even if.
ēveniō, -īre, -vēnī, -ventum (*v.i.*) **:** to turn out.
ēventus, -ūs (*m.*) **:** outcome, result; **ex eventu navium suarum:** from what happened to the ships.
ēvocō, -āre, -āvī, -ātum (*v.t.*) **:** to summon, call out.
exanimō, -āre, -āvī, -ātum (*v.t.*) **:** to kill.
exardescō, -escere, -arsī, -arsum (*v.i.*) **:** to blaze up (fig.).
exaudiō, -īre, -īvī, -ītum (*v.t.*) **:** to hear (from a distance or despite difficulties).
excēdō, -ere, -cessī, -cessum (*v.i.*) **:** to go out, leave.
excellō, -ere, -uī (*v.i.*) **:** to excel, be eminent.
excipiō, -ere, -cēpī, -ceptum (*v.t.*) **:** to catch, meet, support. relieve.
excitō, -āre, -āvī, -ātum (*v.t.*) **:** to raise, kindle, incite.
exclūdō, -ere, -clūsī, -clūsum (*v.t.*) **:** to shut out, cut off, hinder.
excōgitō, -āre, -āvī, -ātum (*v.t.*) **:** to think of, contrive.
excūsō, -āre, -āvī, -ātum (*v.t.* with **se**) **:** apologise for.
exeō, -īre, -iī, -itum (*v.i.*) **:** to go out.

exercitātiō, -ōnis (*f.*) : training, practice.
exercitus, -ūs (*m.*) : army.
exiguitās, -ātis (*f.*) : smallness, fewness.
exiguus, -a, -um : small, scanty.
existimō, -āre, -āvī, -ātum (*v.t.*) : to think, believe.
expedītiō, -ōnis (*f.*) : foray, raid (*i.e.* a task assigned to **expediti**).
expedītus, -a, -um : light armed, unencumbered; see note on ch. II, l. 15; **navium motus ad usum expeditior erat** : the ships were easier to handle.
expellō, -ere, -pulī, -pulsum (*v.t.*) : to drive out.
experior, -īrī, -pertus sum (*v.t.*) : to try.
explōrātor, -ōris (*m.*) : scout, spy, patrol.
explōrō, -āre, -āvī, -ātum (*v.t.*) : to reconnoitre, assure.
expōnō, -ere, -posuī, -positum (*v.t.*) : to explain; **e navibus exponere** : to land.
exsistō, -ere, -stitī, -stitum (*v.i.*) : to stand out, arise, break out.
exspectō, -āre, -āvī, -ātum (*v.t.* and *i.*) : to await, wait.
exstinguō, -ere, -nxī, -nctum (*v.t.*) : to quench, extinguish.
exstō, -āre, -stitī (*v.i.*) : to stand out, project.
exstruō, -ere, -struxī, -structum (*v.t.*) : to erect.
exsul, -ulis (*c.*) : exile.
extrā (*prep.* with *acc.*) : outside.
extrahō, -ere, -traxī, -tractum (*v.t.*) : to protract, spin out.
extrēmus, -a, -um : most distant, the end of, last, extreme, rear.
exuō, -ere, -uī, -ūtum (*v.t.*) : to strip, despoil.

faber, -rī (*m.*) : smith, army mechanic.
facilis, -e : easy.
facinus, -oris (*n.*) : crime, guilt.
faciō, -ere, fēcī, factum (*v.t.*) : to do, make; **iter facere** : to march; **certiorem facere** : to inform.
factiō, -ōnis (*f.*) : faction, party.
factum, -ī (*n.*) : act, exploit.
facultās, -ātis (*f.*) : opportunity
fāgus, -ī (*f.*) : beech-tree.
falsus, -a, -um (*adj.*) : false.
fāma, -ae (*f*) : news, report, fame.
famēs, -is (*f.*) : hunger, famine.
familiāris, -e (*adj.*) : one's own; (usually as *subst.*) intimate friend.
familiāritās, -ātis (*f.*) : friendship.
fās (*indecl., n.*) : right.
fēlīciter (*adv.*) : fortunately, well.
ferē (*adv.*) : almost, generally.
femur, -oris or **-inis** (*n.*) : a thigh.
fera, -ae (*f.*) : wild animal.
ferō, ferre, tulī, lātum (*v.t.*) : to carry, bring, endure; **ut fert illorum opinio . . .** : according to their opinion . . .; **aegre ferre** : to be annoyed at.
ferrāmentum, -ī (*n.*) : iron tool.
ferreus, -a, -um : of iron, iron.
ferrum, -ī (*n.*) : iron.
fertilis, -e (*adj.*) : fertile.
fervefactus, -a, -um (*adj.*) : heated, made red hot.
ferveō, -ēre, -vuī (*v.i.*) : to be aglow, red hot.
fidēlis, -e : faithful, loyal.

fidēs, -ēī (*f.*) : faith, loyalty, protection; **fidem dare** : to pledge one's word; **in fide manere** : to remain loyal; **in fidem recipere** : to admit under one's protection; **fidem interponere** (ch. XXXVI) : to pledge one's word; **fidei faciendae causa** (ch. XLI) : to inspire credit.
figūra, -ae (*f.*) : shape, form.
fīlius, -ī (*m.*) : son.
fīniō, -īre, -īvī, -ītum (*v.t.*) : to limit, define.
fīnis, -is (*m.*) : end; (*pl.*) frontier, territory.
fīnitimus, -a, -um : neighbouring; (as *subst.*) neighbour.
fīō, fierī, factus sum (*v.i.*) : to happen, become, be done.
firmiter (*adv.*) : firmly.
firmus, -a, -um : strong, stable.
flamma, -ae (*f.*) : flame.
flectō, -ere, -xī, -xum (*v.t.*) : to turn, bend.
flētus, -ūs (*m.*) : weeping, wailing.
flō, flāre, flāvī, flātum (*v.i.*) : to blow.
fluctus, -ūs (*m.*) : wave.
flūmen, -inis (*n.*) : river, current.
forma, -ae (*f.*) : shape.
forte (*abl.* of **fors,** used as *adv.*) : by chance.
fortis, -e : strong, brave.
fortiter, -tius, -tissimē (*adv.*) : bravely, resolutely.
fortūna, -ae (*f.*) : fortune; (*pl.*) possessions.
fossa, -ae (*f.*) : ditch, trench.
frangō, -ere, frēgī, fractum (*v.t.*) : to break, wreck.
frāter, -tris (*m.*) : brother.
fremitus, -ūs (*m.*) : hubbub, din.
frīgus, -oris (*n.*) : cold.
frons, -tis (*f.*) : the forehead.
frūmentārius, -a, -um : belonging to corn or provisions; **res frumentaria** : food supplies.
frūmentor, -ārī, -ātus sum (*v.i.*) : to forage, look for corn.
frūmentum, -ī (*n.*) : corn, grain; (*pl.*) standing corn, crops.
frustrā (*adv.*) : in vain.
fuga, -ae (*f.*) : flight, rout, escape.
fugiō, -ere, fūgī, fugitum (*v.t.* and *i.*) : to avoid, flee.
fūmus, -ī (*m.*) : smoke.
funda, -ae (*f.*) : sling.
fundō, -ere, fūdī, fūsum (*v.t.*) : to rout, scatter.
fūnis, -is (*m.*) : rope, cable.
fūsilis, -e (*adj.*) : molten, fluid.

gallīna, -ae (*f.*) : hen, fowl.
gener, -erī (*m.*) : son-in-law.
gens, -ntis (*f.*) : clan, tribe, people.
genus, -eris (*n.*) : kind, class, family.
gerō, -ere, gessī, gestum (*v.t.*) : to carry on, do; **rem gerere** : to manage the business.
gladius, -ī (*m.*) : sword.
glans, -dis (*f.*) : acorn, bullet.
glōria, -ae (*f.*) : glory, renown.
grātia, -ae (*f.*) : influence, favour; **gratiam habere** : to be grateful.
grātulātiō, -ōnis (*f.*) : congratulation, rejoicing.
grātus, -a, -um (*adj.*) : acceptable, pleasing.
gravis, -e : heavy, severe.
gravitās, -ātis (*f.*) : weight.
graviter, gravius, gravissimē (*adv.*) : heavily, seriously, severely; **graviter ferre** : to be annoyed at.

gubernātor, -ōris (*m.*) : helmsman, pilot.
gustō, -āre, -āvī, -ātum (*v.t.*) : to taste.

habēō, -ēre, -uī, -itum (*v.t.*) : to have, hold, consider; **magni habere** : to consider of great importance.
haud (*adv.*) : not.
hērēditās, -ātis (*f.*) : an inheritance.
hīberna, -orum (*n.*) : winter-quarters.
hīc (*adv.*) : here.
hīc, haec, hōc : this.
hiemō, -āre, -āvī, -ātum (*v.i.*) : to winter.
hiems, hiemis (*f.*) : winter, storm, bad weather.
homō, -inis (*m.*) : man, human being.
honor, -ōris (*m.*) : honour, esteem.
hōra, -ae (*f.*) : hour.
horridus, -a, -um : wild.
hortor, -ārī, -ātus sum (*v.t.*) : to harangue, urge, encourage.
hospes, -itis (*m.*) : guest, friend.
hospitium, -ī (*n.*) : ties of hospitality, hospitable relations.
hostis, -is (*m.*) : enemy.
hūc (*adv.*) : hither, to this.
hūmānus, -a, -um : civilised.
humilis, -e : low, shallow.
humilitās, -ātis (*f.*) : low build (of ship), lowness, weakness.

iaciō, -ere, iēcī, iactum (*v.t.*) : to throw.
iactūra, -ae (*f.*) : loss, expenditure.
iaculum, -ī (*n.*) : javelin.
iam (*adv.*) : new, already.
ibi (*adv.*) : there.
idcircō (*adv.*) : on that account, for that reason.
īdem, eadem, idem : same; **idem qui, idem atque** : the same as.
idōneus, -a, -um : suitable, serviceable, convenient.
ignis, -is (*m.*) : fire.
ignōbilis, -e (*adj.*) : obscure.
ignōrō, -āre, -āvī, -ātum (*v.t.*) : to be unaware, not to know.
ignoscō, -ere, -nōvī, -nōtum (*v.i.*, with *dat.*) : to pardon, grant an amnesty.
ignōtus, -a, -um : unknown.
ille, -a, -ud : that, he, she, it, etc.
illō (*adv.*) : thither, to that place.
immānis, -e (*adj.*) : vast, enormous.
immittō, -ere, -mīsī, -missum (*v.t.*) : to let in, send against.
impedimentum, -ī (*n.*) : hindrance; (*pl.*) : baggage.
impediō, -īre, -īvī or **iī, -ītum** (*v.t.*) : to hamper, obstruct; **impedītus** : encumbered, impenetrable, preoccupied.
impellō, -ere, -pulī, -pulsum (*v.t.*) : to urge, instigate.
imperātor, -ōris (*m.*) : general, commander-in-chief.
imperītus, -a, -um : inexperienced, unacquainted with.
imperium, -ī (*n.*) : command, authority; **summa imperi** : chief command.
imperō, -āre, -āvī, -ātum (*v.t.* and *i.*, with *acc.*) : to levy, requisition; (with *dat.*) to command, order.
impetrō, -āre, -āvī, -ātum (*v.t.*) : to gain one's consent, get consent.
impetus, -ūs (*m.*) : attack, rush, fury.

impius, -a, -um (*adj.*): impious; without respect for gods, country, or parents.
implōrō, -āre, -āvī, -ātum (*v.t.*): to beseech, solicit.
importō, -āre, -āvī, -ātum (*v.t.*): to import, bring in.
imprōvīsus, -a, -um: unforeseen; **de improviso**: unexpectedly.
imprūdens, -entis (*adj.*): off one's guard.
imprūdentia, -ae (*f.*): ignorance, short-sightedness.
in (*prep.* (i) with *acc.*): to, towards, into, against; **in altitudinem**: in depth; **in dies**: day by day; **in singulos annos**: annually; (*prep.* (ii) with *abl.*) in, on, among; **in ancoris**: at anchor.
inānis, -e: empty, idle.
incendium, -ī (*n.*): fire.
incendō, -ere, -dī, -sum (*v.t.*): to set fire to.
incertus, -a, -um: vague, ill-defined; **incertis ordinibus**: with ranks disorganised.
incidō, -ere, -cidī, -cāsum (*v.i.*): to fall on, to happen.
incipiō, -ere, -cēpī, -cēptum (*v.t.*): to begin.
incognitus, -a, -um: unknown.
incolō, -ere, -coluī, -cultum, (*v.t.* and *i.*): to inhabit, dwell.
incolumis, -e: safe, unhurt.
incommodē (*adv.*): disastrously.
incommodum, -ī (*n.*): disaster, loss.
incrēdibilis, -e (*adj.*): incredible, marvellous.
incursiō, -ōnis (*f.*): raid, attack.
inde (*adv.*): thence, then.
indīcō, -ere, -dīxī, -dictum (*v.t.*): to appoint, fix, declare.
indignus, -a, -um (*adj.*): unworthy.
ineō, -īre, -iī, -itum (*v.t.*): to enter, begin; **consilium inire**: to form a plan.
infāmia, -ae (*f.*): disgrace.
inferior, -ius (*comp. adj.*): lower, (*superl.*) **infimus.**
inferō, -ferre, -tulī, -latum (*v.t.*): to bring to; **bellum inferre**: to attack.
inficiō, -ere, -fēcī, -fectum (*v.t.*): to stain, dye.
infīnītus, -a, -um: immense.
infirmus, -a, -um: weak, unsound.
infrā (*adv.*): below.
ingens, -ntis (*adj.*): great, immense.
ingredior, -gredī, -gressus sum (*v.i.*): to go into, penetrate.
inimīcitia, -ae (*f.*): feud, enmity.
inimīcus, -a, -um: hostile; (*subst.*) enemy, opponent.
inīquus, -a, -um: unequal, unfavourable, unjust.
initium, -ī (*n.*): beginning.
iniūria, -ae (*f.*): wrong, outrage; (*abl.*) wrongfully, unjustly.
inligō, -āre, -āvī, -ātum (*v.t.*): to fasten on, tie on.
innocens, -utis (*adj.*): innocent.
inopia, -ae (*f.*): want, scarcity.
inquam (*def. v.*): say.
insciens, -ntis (*adj.*): unaware, not knowing.
insequor, -ī, -secūtus sum (*v.t.*): to follow close, pursue.
insidiae, -ārum (*f. pl.*): ambush, trap.
insinuō, -āre, -āvī, -ātum (*v.t.* with **se**): to penetrate.

insistō, -ere, -stitī (*v.i.*) : to stand on, get a footing.
instabilis, -e : unsteady, uncertain.
instigō, -āre, -āvī, -ātum (*v.t.*) : to urge on, incite.
instituō, -ere, -uī, -ūtum (*v.t.*) : to set up, construct, arrange, prepare, begin.
institūtum, -i (*n.*) : custom, institution, practice.
instō, -āre, -stitī (*v.i.*) : to press forward.
instrūmentum, -ī (*n.*) : equipment.
instruō, -ere, -struxī, -structum (*v.t.*) : draw up, equip, build.
insuēfactus, -a, -um : trained, accustomed.
insuētus, -a, -um (with *gen.*) : unaccustomed to.
insula, -ae (*f.*) : island.
integer, -gra, -grum : fresh, unharmed.
intellegō, -ere, -lexī, -lectum (*v.t.*) : to learn, know, perceive.
inter (*prep.* with *acc.*) : among, between; **cohortari inter se** : encourage one another.
intercēdō, -ere, -cessī, -cessum (*v.i.*) : to pass between, intervene, elapse.
intercipiō, -ere, -cēpī, -ceptum (*v.t.*) : to cut off, intercept.
interclūdō, -ere, -clūsī, -clūsum (*v.t.*) : to cut off, shut off, block.
interdicō, -ere, -dīxī, -dictum (*v.t.*) : to forbid, exclude.
intereā (*adv.*) : meanwhile.
interficiō, -ere, -fēcī, -fectum (*v.t.*) : to kill.
interim (*adv.*) : meanwhile.
interior, -ius (*comp. adj.*) : inside, inner.
intermittō, -ere, -mīsī, -missum (*v.t.*) : to let pass, interrupt, leave a gap; **vento intermisso** : the wind having dropped; **brevi tempore intermisso** : after a short interval.
interest : it is important to.
interpōnō, -ere, -posuī, -positum (*v.t.*) : to interpose, put forward; **fidem interponere** : to give one's pledged word.
interpres, -etis (*m.*) : interpreter.
interpretor, -ārī, -ātus sum (*v.t.*) : to explain, expound.
intersum, -esse, -fuī (*v.i.*) : to be present, take part in; **interest** (*impers.*) : it is important to.
intervallum, -ī (*n.*) : interval.
intra (*prep.* with *acc.*) : within, inside.
introitus, -ūs (*m.*) : entrance.
intrōmittō, -ere, -mīsī, -missum (*v.t.*) : to send inside, let in.
intrōrumpō, -ere, -rūpī, -ruptum (*v.i.*) : to break in, enter by force.
intus (*adv.*) : inside, within.
inūsitātus, -a, -um : unfamiliar, strange.
inūtilis, -e : useless.
inveniō, -īre, -vēnī, ventum (*v.t.*) : to find, learn.
inventor, -ōris (*m.*) : author, discoverer.
invītō, -āre, -āvī, -ātum (*v.t.*) : to lure on, tempt.
ipse, -a, -um : self, very, in person.
is, ea, id : that, this, he, she, it, etc.
ita (*adv.*) : so, thus.
itaque (*conj.*) : and so, accordingly.
item (*adv.*) : likewise, besides.

iter, itineris (*n.*): journey, march; **labore atque itinere**: by hard marching.
iubeō, -ēre, iussī, iussum (*v.t.*): to order.
iūdicium, -ī (*n.*): trial, judgment, decision.
iūdicō, -āre, -āvī, -ātum (*v.t.*): to judge, decide, suppose.
iūmentum, -ī (*n.*): draught animal, horse, ox.
iūrō, -āre, -āvī, -ātum (*v.i.*): to swear.
iūs, iūris (*n.*): right; **ius iurandum**: oath.
iustitia, -ae (*f.*): justice.
iustus, -a, -um (*adj.*): just, regular, proper.
iuvō, -āre, iūvī, iūtum (*v.t.*): to help.

L: Lucius (Roman *praenomen*): 50.
lābor, -ī, lapsus sum (*v.t.*): to fall, to revolt.
labor, -ōris (*m.*): work, toil, hardship.
labōrō, -āre, -āvī, -ātum (*v.i.*): to toil, be hard pressed.
lăbrum, -ī (*n.*): lip.
lāc, lactis (*n.*): milk.
lacessō, -ere, -īvī, -ītum (*v.t.*): to harass, challenge.
laetitia, -ae (*f.*): exultation, rejoicing.
languor, -oris (*m.*): feebleness, exhaustion.
lapis, -idis (*m.*): a stone.
largior, -īrī, -ītus sum (*v.t.*): to bestow, give generously.
lātē, -ius, -issimē (*adv.*): widely, far and wide.
lātitūdō, -inis (*f.*): width, breadth.
latus, -eris (*n.*): side, flank.
lātus, -a, -um: broad.
laudō, -āre, -āvī, -ātum (*v.t.*): to praise.
laus, -dis (*f.*): praise, renown, credit.
lēgātiō, -ōnis (*f.*): mission, embassy.
lēgātus, -ī (*m.*): (i) envoy; (ii) military officer under the commander-in-chief.
legiō, -ōnis (*f.*): legion.
legiōnārius, -a, -um: legionary.
lēnis, -e: gentle, moderate.
lepus, -oris (*m.*): hare.
levis, -e (*adj.*): light; hence light-minded, puerile, undignified.
levitās, -ātis (*f.*): lightness.
levō, -āre, -āvī, -ātum (*v.t.*): to ease, relieve of, free from.
lex, lēgis (*f.*): law.
līber, -era, -erum: free.
līberāliter (*adv.*): graciously, kindly.
līberī, -ōrum (*m. pl.*): children.
līberō, -āre, -āvī, -ātum (*v.t.*): set free, release.
lībertās, -ātis (*f.*): liberty, freedom.
licet, -uit and **licitum est** (*v.i.*): it is lawful, allowed.
lignātiō, -ōnis (*f.*): getting wood for fuel.
lignātor, -ōris (*m.*): wood-cutter.
līs, lītis (*f.*): lawsuit, matter in dispute; **litem aestimare**: to assess damages.
litterae, -ārum (*f. pl.*): letter, dispatch; **litterae publicae**: official documents.
lītus, -oris (*n.*): shore.
locus, -ī (*m.*): place, position; **obsidum loco**: as hostages.
longē, -ius, -issimē (*adv.*): far, far off.
longinquus, -a, -um: distant.

longitūdō, -inis (*f.*) : length.
longus, -a, -um : long; **navis longa** : warship.
loquor, -ī, locūtus sum (*v.t.* and *i.*) : to speak.
lōrīca, -ae (*f.*) : cuirass; breast-work, parapet.
lūna, -ae (*f.*) : moon.
lux, lūcis (*f.*) : light, dawn; **prima luce** : at daybreak.

M : Marcus (Roman *praenomen*).
magistrātus, -ūs (*m.*) : magistrate, office.
magnificus, -a, -um : (*adj.*) splendid.
magnopere, magis, maximē (*adv.*) : greatly.
magnus, -a, -um : great, important; **magni habere** : to value highly; **voce magna** : in a loud voice; **maiores** : ancestors.
male (*adv.*) : badly.
mandātum, -ī (*n.*) : order, instructions.
mandō, -āre, -āvī, -ātum (*v.t.*) : to instruct, order, entrust; **se fugae mandare** : to take to flight.
māne (*adv.*) : in the morning.
maneō, -ēre, mansī, mansum (*v.i.*) : to remain.
manus, -ūs (*f.*) : hand, body of troops; **dat manus** : gives away; when contrasted with **natura**, it means art, human skill.
mare, -is (*n.*) : the sea; **mare nostrum** : the Mediterranean.
maritimus, -a, -um : belonging to the sea, maritime.
mās, maris (*adj.*) : male.
māteria, -ae (*f.*) : timber.
mātūrus, -a, -um : ripe.
medeor, -ērī, meditus sum (*v.i.*, with *dat.*) : to remedy.
mediōcris, -e (*adj.*) : ordinary, moderate.
mediterrāneus, -a, -um : inland.
medius, -a, -um : middle.
membrum, -ī (*n.*) : limb.
memoria, -ae (*f.*) : memory, record.
mensis, -is (*m.*) : month.
mensūra, -ae (*f.*) : measurement.
mercātor, -ōris (*m.*) : trader, merchant.
mercātūra, -ae (*f.*) : commerce.
merīdiānus, -a, -um : of midday.
merīdiēs, -ēī (*m.*) : midday, south.
meritum, -ī (*n.*) : service, desert.
metō, -ere, messuī, messum (*v.t.*) : to reap.
metus, -ūs (*m.*) : fear.
meus, -a, -um : my, mine.
mīles, -itis (*m.*) : soldier.
mīlitāris, -e : military; **res militaris** : the art of war.
mīlitia, -ae (*f.*) : military service.
mille : 1000; **mille** (*sc.* **passuum**) : mile.
minimē (*superl. adv.*) : by no means.
minor, minus (*comp. adj.*) : less.
minuō, -ere, -uī, -ūtum (*v.t.*) : to lessen, weaken, settle (a dispute).
mīror, -ārī, -ātus sum (*v.t.*) : to be surprised, wonder at.
missus, -ūs (*m.*, only in *abl.*) : a sending; **missu Caesaris** : sent by Caesar.
mittō, -ere, mīsī, missum (*v.t.*) : to send, throw (weapons).

modo (*adv.*): merely, only, lately.
modus, -ī (*m.*): manner, kind, size.
mollis, -e: soft; ch. IX: sandy, gently sloping.
moneō, -ēre, -uī, -itum (*v.t.*): to warn, advise.
mons, -ntis (*m.*): mountain, hill.
mora, -ae (*f.*): delay.
morbus, -ī (*m.*): disease.
morior, -ī, mortuus sum (*v.i.*): to die.
moror, -ārī, -ātus sum (*v.t.* and *i.*): to halt, delay.
mors, -rtis (*f.*): death.
mōs, mōris (*m.*): custom.
mōtus, -ūs (*m.*): movement, disturbance.
moveō, -ēre, mōvī, mōtum (*v.t.*): to move.
multitūdō, -inis (*f.*): multitude, number.
multus, -a, -um: much, many.
mūnīmentum, -ī (*n.*): barrier, protection.
mūniō, -īre, -īvī, -ītum (*v.t.*): to fortify.
mūnītiō, -ōnis (*f.*): entrenchments, fortification.
mūnus, -eris (*n.*): a duty, present.
mūrālis, -e (*adj.*): mural; **pilum murale**: heavy pike used in the defence of walls.
mūrus, -ī (*m.*): wall, rampart.

nam (*conj.*): for.
namque (*conj.*): for indeed, for.
nanciscor, -ī, nactus sum (*v.t.*): to get, obtain.
nascor, -ī, nātus sum (*v.i.*): to be born, to be found; (*subst.*) **natus**: child, son.
nātiō, -ōnis (*f.*): nation, tribe.
nātūra, -ae (*f.*): nature, character.
nauta, -ae (*f.*): sailor.
nāvālis, -e: nautical, naval.
nāvigātiō, -ōnis (*f.*): navigation, sailing, voyage.
nāvigium, -ī (*n.*): galley.
nāvigō, -āre, -āvī, -ātum (*v.t.*): to sail.
nāvis, -is (*f.*): ship.
nē (*adv.* and *conj.*): (i) (*adv.*) not; (ii) (*adv.*) **ne . . . quidem**: not even; ch. XLIV, of course . . . not . . .; (iii) (*conj.*) lest; that not.
-ne: enclitic, introducing a question.
nec: see **neque.**
necessārius, -a, -um: necessary.
necesse (*indecl. adj.*): necessary.
necessitās, -ātis (*f.*): necessity, exigencies.
necō, -āre, -āvī, -ātum (*v.t.*): to put to death.
neglegō, -ere, -lexī, -lectum (*v.t.*): to neglect, disregard, overlook.
negō, -āre, -āvī, -ātum (*v.t.*): to deny, say . . . not, refuse.
negōtium, -ī (*n.*): business, undertaking, trouble; **nihil esse negotii** (ch. XXXVIII): it is not a difficult matter.
nēmō (*irreg.*): no one, nobody.
nēquāquam (*adv.*): by no means.
neque or **nec** (*conj.*): nor, and not; **neque . . . neque**: neither . . . nor.
nervus, -ī (*m.*): sinew; (*pl.*) strength, vigour.
neu, neve (*conj.*) = **et ne.**
nex, necis (*f.*): death, execution.
nihil (*indecl. n.*): nothing, not.
nihilō (*abl.* of **nihilum**): none.
nisi (*conj.*): unless, if not, except.

nītor, -ī, nīsus or **nīxus sum** (*v.i.*) : to strive.
nōbilis, -e : noble, of high rank.
nōbilitās, -ātis (*f.*) : high birth, nobility.
noceō, -ēre, -uī, -ītum (*v.i.*) : to hurt, injure.
noctū (*adv.*): by night.
nocturnus, -a, -um : nightly, in the night.
nōdus, -ī (*m.*) : knot, joint (of body).
nōlō, nolle, nōluī (*v.i.*) : to be unwilling.
nōmen, -inis (*n.*) : name.
nōminātim (*adv.*) : by name, individually.
nōn (*adv.*) : not.
nondum (*adv.*) : not yet.
nōnus, -a, -um : ninth.
nōs : we.
noscō, -ere, nōvī, nōtum (*v.t.*) : to get to know; (*perf.*) to know.
noster, -ra, -rum : our; **nostri** : our men, *i.e.* Romans.
nōtitia, -ae (*f.*) : knowledge.
nōtus, -a, -um : known, well-known.
novem : nine.
novitās, -ātis (*f.*) : novelty, strangeness.
novus, -a, -um : new; **novissimus** : last, rear.
nox, noctis (*f.*) : night.
nūdō, -āre, -āvī, -ātum (*v.t.*) : to uncover, make bare, expose.
nūdus, -a, -um (*adj.*) : bare, exposed.
nullus, -a, -um : no, none; **non nullus** : some.
nūmen, -inis (*n.*) : will, spirit (of the gods).
numerus, -ī (*m.*) : number.
nummus, -ī (*m.*) : coin.
nunquam (*adv.*) : never; **non nunquam** (*adv.*) : sometimes.
nunc (*adv*) : now.
nuntiō, -āre, -āvī, -ātum (*v.t.*) : to announce, tell.
nuntius, -iī (*m.*) : messenger, news.
nūtus, -ūs (*m.*) : nod, intimation; **ad nutum** : smartly, at the least intimation.

ob (*prep.* with *acc.*) : on account of.
obeō, -īre, -īvī, -itum (*v.i.*) : to attend to.
obiciō, -ere, -iēcī, -iectum (*v.t.*) : to throw in the way, set as an obstacle.
observō, -āre, -āvī, -ātum (*v.t.*) : to watch, obey, reckon.
obses, -idis (*m.*) : hostage.
obsideō, -ēre, -sēdī, -sessum (*v.t.*) : to besiege, beset.
obsidiō, -ōnis (*f.*) : siege, blockade.
obstinātē (*adv.*) : steadily, stubbornly.
obstruō, -ere, -struxī, -structum (*v.t.*) : to block up.
obtemperō, -āre, -āvī, -ātum (*v.i.* with *dat.*) : to obey.
obtineō, -ēre, -tinuī, -tentum (*v.t.*) : to hold, occupy.
occāsiō, -ōnis (*f.*) : opportunity.
occāsus, -ūs (*m.*) : setting; **solis occasus** : sunset, west.
occīdō, -ere, -cidī (*v.i.*) : to fall; **(sol) occidens** : the west.
occīdō, -ere, -cīdī, -cīsum (*v.t.*) : to kill.
occulō, -ere, -luī, -cultum (*v.t.*) : to hide.
occultō, -āre, -āvī, -ātum (*v.t.*) : to hide.

occupō, -āre, -āvī, -ātum (*v.t.*) : to seize; **occupatus** : busy.
occurrō, -ere, -currī, -cursum (*v.i.*) : to face, meet an attack.
ōcius (*comp. adv.*) : more quickly.
octāvus, -a, -um : eighth.
octingentī, -ae, -a : 800.
octō : eight.
octōgintā : eighty.
oculus, -ī (*m.*) : eye.
officium, -ī (*n.*) : loyalty, duty, service; **officium praestare** (ch. XXXIII) : to do one's duty.
omnīnō (*adv.*) : altogether, at all.
omnis, -e : all, every.
onerārius, -a, -um : carrying freight; **navis oneraria** : transport.
onerō, -āre, -āvī, -ātum (*v.t.*) : to load.
onus, -eris (*n.*) : load, burden.
opera, -ae (*f.*) : exertion, trouble, attention.
opīniō, -ōnis (*f.*) : expectation, impression, belief.
oportet, -ēre, -uit (*impers.*) : it is necessary, it behoves.
oppidum, -ī (*n.*) : town, stronghold.
opportūnus, -a, -um : suitable.
opprimō, -ēre, -pressī, -pressum (*v.t.*) : to crush, overpower, surprise.
oppugnātiō, -ōnis (*f.*) : attack, assault.
oppugnō, -āre, -āvī, -ātum (*v.t.*) : to attack, storm, besiege.
(ops), opis (*f.*) : help; (*pl.*) power, resources.
optimus, -a, -um : best.
opus, -eris (*m.*) : work; (*pl.*) military works, siege-works, trenches, etc.; **opus est** : there is need of.
ōra, -ae (*f.*) : shore, coast.
ōrātiō, -ōnis (*f.*) : speech.
ōrātor, -ōris (*m.*) : spokesman, envoy.
orbis, -is (*m.*) : circle, hollow square.
ordō, -inis (*m.*) : row, rank, grade.
orior, -īrī, ortus sum (*v.i.*) : to arise; (**sol**) **oriens** : the east, sunrise.
ōrō, -āre, -āvī, -ātum (*v.t.*) : to beg, pray.
ōs, ōris (*n.*) : mouth, face.
ostendō, -ere, -dī, -sum and **-tum** (*v.t.*) : to show, point out.
ostentō, -āre, -āvī, -ātum (*v.t.*) : to display, point to.

pābulātor, -ōris (*fim.*) : forager.
pābulor, -ārī, -ātus sum (*v.i.*) : to forage.
pācō, -āre, -āvī, -ātum (*v.t.*) : to tranquillize, subdue.
paene (*adv.*) : almost, nearly.
pāgus, -ī (*m.*) : country district, village.
palam (*adv.*) : openly.
palūs, -ūdis (*f.*) : marsh, swamp.
pār, paris (*adj.*) : equal.
parcō, -ere, pepercī and **parsī, parsum** (*v.i.*) : to spare.
parens, -ntis (*c.*) : parent.
pāreō, -ēre, -uī, -itum (*v.i.*, with *dat.*) : to obey.
pariō, -ere, peperī, partum (*v.t.*): to win, gain, secure.
parō, -āre, -āvī, -ātum (*v.t.*) : to prepare.
pars, -rtis (*f.*) : part, direction.
partim (*adv.*) : partly.
parvulus, -a, -um (*adj.*) : small, young.
passus, -ūs (*m.*) : pace; **mille passus** : a mile.

pateō, -ere, -uī (*v.i.*) : to lie open, extend, stretch.
pater, -tris (*m.*) : father.
patientia, -ae (*f.*) : patience.
patior, patī, passus sum (*v.t.*) : to suffer, endure, allow.
paucitās, -ātis (*f.*) : scarcity, scanty numbers.
paucus, -a, -um : few.
paulātim (*adv.*) : little by little, by degrees.
paulisper (*adv.*) : for a short time.
paulō and **paulum** (*adv.*) : from **paulus, -a, -um** : a little, somewhat.
pax, pācis (*f.*) : peace.
pectus, -oris (*n.*) : breast.
pecūnia, -ae (*f.*) : money.
pecus, -oris (*n.*) : cattle.
pedes, -itis (*m.*) : foot-soldier, infantryman.
peditātus, -ūs (*m.*) : infantry.
pellis, -is (*f.*) : skin, hide.
pellō, -ere, pepulī, pulsum (*v.t.*) : to beat off, put to flight.
pendō, -ere, pependī, pensum (*v.t.*) : to pay, weigh.
per (*prep.* with *acc.*) : by means of, through, along.
peragō, -ere, -ēgī, -actum (*v.t.*) : to perform, finish.
percipiō, -ere, -cēpī, -ceptum (*v.t.*) : to take note of, hear, listen to.
percontātiō, -ōnis (*f.*) : inquiry.
percurrō, -ere, -currī, -cursum (*v.t.* and *i.*) : to run along.
percutiō, -ere, -cussī, -cussum (*v.t.*) : to strike, pierce.
perdiscō, -ere, -didicī (*v.t.*) : to learn by heart.
perdūcō, -ere, -duxī, -ductum (*v.t.*) : to bring, win over, prolong.
perendinus, -a, -um (*adj.*) : after to-morrow.
pereō, -īre, -iī, -itum (*v.i.*) : to perish, be killed.
perexiguus, -a, -um : very small.
perferō, -ferre, -tulī, -lātum (*v.t.*) : to spread abroad, deliver (letters).
perficiō, -ere, -fēcī, -fectum (*v.t.*) : to finish, achieve.
perfuga, -ae (*f.*) : deserter.
perfugiō, -ere, -fūgī (*v.i.*) : to desert, flee for refuge.
perīclum, -ī (*n.*) : (i) trial, attempt; (ii) risk, danger.
perlegō, -ere, -lēgī, -lectum (*v.t.*) : to read through.
permaneō, -ēre, -mansī, -mansum (*v.i.*) : to remain, continue.
permittō, -ere, -mīsī, -missum (*v.t.*) : to allow, authorise, entrust.
permoveō, -ēre, -mōvī, -mōtum (*v.t.*) : to move deeply, sway, overbear.
perpaucus, -a, -um : very few.
perpetuus, -a, -um : lasting, continuous, unbroken; **in perpetuum** : for ever.
perrumpō, -ere, -rūpī, -ruptum (*v.t.* and *i.*) : to break through.
persequor, -ī, -secūtus sum (*v.t.*) : to pursue.
perseverō, -āre, -āvī, -ātum (*v.i.*) : to persist.
perspiciō, -ere, -spexī, spectum (*v.t.*) : to see clearly, reconnoitre, realise.
persuādeō, -ēre, -suasī, -suāsum (*v.t.*, with *dat.*) : to persuade, induce.
perterreō, -ēre, -uī, -itum (*v.t.*) : to frighten, demoralise.
pertinācia, -ae (*f.*) : obstinacy.

pertineō, -ēre, -tinuī, -tentum (*v.i.*): to pertain, tend, extend; **ad plures pertinebat** (ch. xxv): a large number of persons were concerned.

perturbō, -āre, -āvī, -ātum (*v.t.*): to throw into confusion, unnerve.

perveniō, -īre, -vēnī, -ventum (*v.i.*): to arrive.

pēs, pedis (*m.*): foot.

petō, -ere, -īvī, -ītum (*v.t.*): to seek, make for, attack.

pietās, -ātis (*f.*): dutiful conduct (*e.g.* to gods, parents, country).

pīlum, -ī (*n.*): heavy javelin (see Pl. VI).

pīlus, -ī (*m.*): a century; **primus pilus**: leading century of a legion.

pinna, -ae (*f.*): pinnacle, battlements.

plācō, -āre, -āvī, -ātum (*v.t.*): to propitiate, appear.

plānus, -a, -um: flat.

plebs, plēbis, (*f.*): populace, the masses.

plēnus, -a, -um: full.

plērīque, pleraeque pleraque: most.

plērumque (*adv.*): generally, for the most part.

plumbum, -ī (*n.*): lead; **plumbum album**: tin.

plūs, plūris: more; (*adv.*) **plus, plurimum**: more, most.

pōculum, -ī (*n.*): drinking-cup.

poena, -ae (*f.*): punishment, penalty.

polliceor, -ērī, -itus sum (*v.t.* and *i.*): to promise, offer.

pollicitātiō, -onis (*f.*): promise, offer.

pondus, -eris (*n.*): weight.

pōnō, -ere, posui, positum (*v.t.*): to place, put; **castra ponere**: to pitch camp.

pons, pontis (*m.*): bridge, causeway.

populor, -ārī, -ātus sum (*v.t.*): to ravage.

populus, -ī (*m.*): people, nation.

porrō (*adv.*): furthermore.

porta, -ae (*f.*): gate.

portō, -āre, -āvī, -ātum (*v.t.*): to carry, take.

portus, -ūs (*m.*): harbour.

poscō, -ere, poposcī (*v.t.*): to demand.

possessiō, -ōnis (*f.*): possession, property.

possum, posse, potuī (*v.i.*): to be able, to have power.

post (i) (*prep.* with *acc.*): after, behind; (ii) (*adv.*) after.

posteā (*adv.*): afterwards; **posteāquam** = **postquam.**

posterus, -a, -um: next, following; (*superl.*) **postremus**: last.

postpōnō, -ere, -posuī, -positum (*v.t.*): to postpone, to make give way.

postquam (*conj.*): when, after.

postremō (*adv.*): lastly.

postrīdiē (*adv.*): on the next day; *sometimes with* **eius diei.**

postulō, -āre, -āvī, -ātum (*v.t.*): to ask for, demand.

potens, -tis (*adj.*): powerful.

potentia, -ae (*f.*): influence.

potestās, -ātis (*f.*): power, opportunity, possibility.

praeceps, -cipitis (*adj.*): steep, headlong.

praecipiō, -ere, -cēpī, -ceptum (*v.t.*): to bid, order, instruct.

praecipuus, -a, -um (*adj.*): special.

praecludō, -ere, -clūsī, -clūsum (*v.t.*): to block, bar, hinder.

praecō, -ōnis (*m.*) : crier, herald.
praeda, -ae (*f.*) : plunder.
praedicō, -āre, -āvī, -ātum (*v.t.*) : to affirm, proclaim.
praedor, -ārī, -ātus sum (*v.i.*) : to plunder.
praeferō, -ferre, -tulī, -lātum (*v.t.*) : to prefer, place before.
praeficiō, -ere, -fēcī, -fectum (*v.t.*) : to place in command, in charge.
praefīgō, -ere, -fixī, -fixum (*v.t.*) : to plant in front.
praemittō, -ere, -mīsī, missum (*v.t.*) : to send ahead.
praemium, -ī (*n.*) : reward.
praeparō, -āre, -āvī, -ātum (*v.t.*) : to prepare, get ready beforehand.
praesens, -ntis : present.
praesentia, -ae (*f.*) : presence.
praesentiō, -īre, -sensī, -sensum (*v.t.*) : to anticipate, get wind of.
praesertim (*adv.*) : especially.
praesidium, -ī (*n.*) : garrison, guard, escort, protection.
praestō (*adv.*) : at hand; **praesto sum** (with *dat.*) : to present oneself before, wait upon.
praestō, -āre, -stitī, -stitum (i) (*v.t.*) : to display, fulfil; **fidem praestare** : to keep a promise; **officium praestare** : to do one's duty; (ii) (*v.i.*) to surpass, excel; **praestat** : it is better.
praesum, -esse, -fuī (*v.i.*) : to be at the head, to command.
praeter (*prep.* with *acc.*) : past, except, beyond.
praetereā (*adv.*) : besides.
praeterquam (*adv.*) : besides, except.
praeūrō, -ere, -ussī, -ustum (*v.t.*) : to burn to a point, burn at the end.
precēs, -um (*f. pl.*) : prayers, entreaties.
premō, -ere, pressī, pressum (*v.t.*) : to press, harass, crush.
prīdiē (*adv.*) : on the day before.
prīmō (*adv.*) : at first.
prīmum (*adv.*) : first; **ubi, cum primum** : as soon as; **quam primum** : as soon as possible.
prīmus, -a, -um : first; **prima luce** : at daybreak; **in primis** : especially; **primi** : the vanguard.
princeps, -cipis : first, leading; (*subst.*) leading man, chieftain.
principātus, -ūs (*m.*) : principal power, supremacy.
prior, -ōris (*comp. adj.*) : former; **priores** : the van.
pristinus, -a, -um : ancient, early.
prius (*adv.*) : before.
priusquam (*conj.*) : before.
prīvātim (*adv.*) : unofficially, as a private person, individually.
prīvātus, -a, -um : private.
prō (*prep.* with *abl.*) : before, for, compared with; **pro sano facere** (ch. VII) : to behave like . . . ; **pro tempore et pro re** : as the time and circumstances might direct; **pro eius iustitia** : in view of.
probō, -āre, -āvī, -ātum (*v.t.*) : to prove, approve, justify.
prōcēdō, -ere, -cessī, -cessum (*v.i.*) : to advance, go forward.
procul (*adv.*) : at a distance, some way off.
prōcumbō, -ere, -cubuī, -cubitum (*v.i.*) : to lie down, sink down, sink to the ground.

prōcūrō, -āre, -āvī, -ātum (*v.t.*) : to look after.
prōcurrō, -ere, -currī, -cursum (*v.i.*) : to run forward, charge.
prōdeō, -īre, -iī, -itum (*v.i.*) : to go forward.
prōditor, -ōris (*m.*) : traitor.
prōdō, -ere, -didī, -ditum (*v.t.*) : to hand down, record, betray.
prōdūcō, -ere, -duxī, -ductum (*v.t.*) : to bring out, belong.
proelior, -iārī, -iātus sum (*v.i.*) : to fight.
proelium, -ī (*n.*) : battle.
profectiō, -ōnis (*f.*) : departure, setting out.
proficiscor, -ī, profectus sum (*v.i.*) : to set out, start.
profiteor, -ērī, -fessus sum (*v.t.*) : to offer, promise, declare.
prōfugiō, -ere, -fūgī (*v.t.*) : to flee, escape.
prōgredior, -ī, -gressus sum (*v.i.*) : to go forward, advance.
prohibeō, -ēre, -uī, -itum (*v.t.*) : to prevent, check, keep away from.
prōiciō, -ere, -iēcī, -iectum (*v.t.*) : to throw, throw away, throw down.
prōmittō, -ere, -mīsī, -missum (*v.t.*) : to let grow long; **promissus**: long.
prōnuntiō, -āre, -āvī, -ātum (*v.t.*) : to announce, declare, give the word.
prope (i) (*prep.* with *acc.*) : near; (ii) (*adv.*) nearly; (*superl.*) **proxime**: recently.
prōpellō, -ere, -pulī, -pulsum (*v.t.*) : to drive before one, drive off.
properō, -āre, -āvī, -ātum (*v.i.*) : to hurry, hasten.
propinquitās, -ātis (*f.*) : nearness, relationship.
propinquus, -a, -um: near, related; **propinqui**: relatives.
prōpōnō, -ere, -posuī, -positum (*v.t.*) : to offer, state, describe.
proprius, -a, -um (*adj.*) : one's own, particular; **proprium** (*subst.*) : characteristic mark, special sign.
propter (*prep.* with *acc.*) : owing to.
propterea quod (*conj.*) : because.
prōpugnō, -āre, -āvī, -ātum (*v.i.*) : to rush out to fight, make sallies, resist.
prōpulsō, -āre, -āvī, -ātum (*v.t.*) : to repel, drive bac.
prōsequor, -ī, -secūtus sum (*v.t.*) : to pursue.
prospectus, -ūs (*m.*) : view, sight.
prospiciō, -ere, -spexī, -spectum (*v.t.* and *i.*) : to look forward, provide for.
prōtegō, -ere, -texī, -tectum (*v.t.*) : to cover, protect.
prōterreō, -ēre, -uī, -itum (*v.t.*) : to frighten away.
prōtinus (*adv.*) : forthwith, at once.
prōvehō, -ere, -vexī, -vectum (*v.t.*) : to carry forward; (*pass.*) (of ships) : to move forward, sail on.
prōveniō, -īre, -venī, -ventum (*v.i.*) : to come up, grow (*e.g.* of corn).
prōvideō, -ēre, -vīdī, -vīsum (*v.t.*) : to foresee, arrange for.
prōvincia, -ae (*f.*) : a province, the Province (*i.e.* in South France).
proximē (*adv.*) : see **prope.**
proximus, -a, -um: neighbouring, next, recent.
pūbes and **pūber, eris** (*adj.*) : grown up, adult; (*pl.*) grown up men.

publicē (*adv.*): officially, on behalf of the government, as a community.
publicō, -āre, -āvī, -ātum (*v.t.*): to confiscate.
publicus, -a, -um: of the state; **publicum consilium**: government policy.
pugna, -ae (*f.*): battle, fight.
pugnō, -āre, -āvī, -ātum (*v.i.*): to fight.
pulvis, -eris (*m.*): dust.
putō, -āre, -āvī, -ātum (*v.t.*): to think, believe, feel.

Q: Quintus (Roman *praenomen*).
quā (*adv.*): where, by which way.
quādrāgintā: forty.
quādringentī, -ae, -a: 400.
quaestiō, -ōnis (*f.*): investigation.
quaestor, -ōris (*m.*): quaestor.
quaestus, -ūs (*m.*): gaining, acquisition.
quam (*adv.*): how, as; **quam prīmum**: as soon as possible; **quam plurimi**: as many as possible.
quantus, -a, -um: how great, how much, as great, as much; **quanto**: by how much, by as much as.
quartus, -a, -um: fourth.
quattuor: four.
-que (*enclitic conj.*): and.
queror, -ī, questus sum (*v.t.* and *i.*): to complain, complain of.
quī, quae, quod (*relat. pron.*): who, which, that.
quīcumque, quaecumque, quodcumque (*relat. pron.*): whoever, whatever.
quīdam, quaedam, quoddam: a certain; (*pl.*) some.
quidem (*conj.*): indeed, but; **ne . . . quidem**: not even.
quiēs, -ētis (*f.*): rest, sleep.
quiētus, -a, -um (*adj.*): peaceful, quiet.
quīn (*conj.*): but that, that not.
quindecim: fifteen.
quingentī, -ae, -a: 500.
quinquāgintā: fifty.
quinque: five.
quis, quid (*interrog. pron.*): what, what; **quid**: why.
quis, qua, quid (*indef. pron.* and *adj.*): any one, any.
quispiam, quaepiam, quidpiam (*indef. pron.*): any, anyone.
quisquam, quaequam, quicquam (*indef. pron.*): any one, anything.
quisque, quaeque, quodque (*indef. pron.*): each, every.
quō (*adv.*): whither.
quoad (*adv.*): until, so long as.
quod (*conj.*): because, that; **quod si**: but if.
quoniam (*conj.*): since, seeing that.
quoque (*conj.*): also.
quot: how many, as many as.
quotannīs (*adv.*): yearly.
quotiens (*adv.*): how often, as often as.

rādix, -īcis (*f.*): root.
rādō, -ere, rāsī, rāsum (*v.t.*): to shave.
rāmus, -ī (*m.*): branch, bough.
rārus, -a, -um: here and there, few at a time.
ratiō, -ōnis (*f.*): reason, way, plan, account.
rebelliō, -ōnis (*f.*): renewal of hostilities.
recēdō, -ere, -cessī, -cessum (*v.i.*): to go back, retire.

recens, -ntis (*adj.*): fresh.
receptus, -ūs (*m.*): retreat, refuge.
recessus, -ūs (*m.*): retreat, means of retreat.
recipiō, -ere, -cēpī, -ceptum (*v.t.*): to take back, get back, recover; **se recipere**: to retreat; **se ex timore recipere**: to rally.
recitō, -āre, -āvī, -ātum (*v.t.*): to read aloud.
reclīnō, -āre, -āvī, -ātum (*v.t.*): to bend back, lean.
recuperō, -āre, -āvī, -ātum (*v.t.*): to recover, win back.
recūsō, -āre, -āvī, -ātum (*v.t.* and *i.*): to shrink from, object, refuse.
reddō, -ere, -didī, -ditum (*v.t.*): to restore, render.
redeō, -īre, -iī, -itum (*v.i.*): to return.
redigō, -ere, -ēgī, -actum (*v.t.*): to reduce, render.
reditus, -ūs (*m.*): return.
redūcō, -ere, -duxī, -ductum (*v.t.*): to bring back, lead back.
referō, -ferre, rettulī, relātum (*v.t.*): to bring back, convey, report; **pedem referre**: to retreat.
reficiō, -ere, -fēcī, -fectum (*v.t.*): to repair.
refugiō, -ere, -fūgī (*v.i.*): to escape.
regiō, -ōnis (*f.*): region, district, direction.
regnō, -āre, -āvī, -ātum (*v.i.*): to reign, be king.
regnum, -ī (*n.*): kingly power, kingdom.
regō, -ere, -xi, -ctum (*v.t.*): to direct, control, rule.
regredior, -ī, -gressus sum (*v.i.*): to go back, retreat.
reiciō, -ere, -iēcī, -iectum (*v.t.*): to drive back, repulse.
relegō, -āre, -āvī, -ātum (*v.t.*): to banish.
rēligiō, -ōnis (*f.*): religious scruple or obligation.
relinquō, -ere, -līquī, -lictum (*v.t.*): to leave, abandon.
reliquus, -a, -um: remaining, left; (*pl. subst.*) the rest.
remaneō, -ēre, -mansī (*v.i.*): to stay behind.
rēmigō, -āre, -āvī, -ātum (*v.i.*): to row.
remigrō, -āre, -āvī, -ātum (*v.i.*): to retire, move back again.
remittō, -ere, -mīsī, -missum (*v.t.*): to send back, stop, relax; **remissus**: mild, not severe; **remittere de celeritate** (ch. XLIX): to slacken speed.
removeō, -ēre, -mōvī, -mōtum (*v.t.*): to dismiss, send away, force back.
rēmus, -ī (*m.*): oar.
renuntiō, -āre, -āvī, -ātum (*v.t.*): to bring back news.
repellō, -ere, reppulī, repulsum (*v.t.*): to drive back, foil; **ab hac spe repulsi** (ch. XLII): foiled in this hope.
repente (*adv.*): suddenly.
repentīnus, -a, -um: sudden, unexpected.
reperiō, -īre, repperī, repertum (*v.t.*): to find.
repetō, -ere, -īvī, -ītum (*v.t.*): to ask back, apply again for.
reportō, -āre, -āvī, -ātum (*v.t.*): to carry back.
reposcō, -ere (*v.t.*): to demand.
reprehendō, -ere, -dī, -sum (*v.t.*): to find fault with, blame.

rēs, rēi (*f.*) : *a word with many meanings, of which the appropriate one must be derived from the context*, e.g. **res maritimae :** seamanship; **res militaris :** the science of war, considerations of tactics; **res publica :** state affairs, republic, the public service (ch. XLVI).
reservō, -āre, -āvī, -ātum (*v.t.*) : to keep, reserve.
resistō, -ere, -stitī (*v.i.*) : to resist, halt, stand one's ground.
respiciō, -ere, -spexī, -spectum (*v.t.* and *i.*) : to look back, have regard to.
respondeō, -ēre, -dī, -sum (*v.i.*) : to reply.
responsum, -ī, (n.) : reply.
restituō, -ere, -uī, -ūtum (*v.t.*) : to restore, rebuild.
retineō, -ēre, -uī, -tentum (*v.t.*) : to hold fast, maintain, preserve.
retrahō, -ere, -traxī, -tractum (*v.t.*) : to bring back.
revertor, -ī, -versus sum (*v.i.*) : to turn back, return.
revocō, -āre, -āvī, -ātum (*v.t.*) : to recall.
rex, rēgis (*m.*) : king.
rīpa, -ae (*f.*) : river-bank.
rīvus, -ī (*m.*) : stream.
rogō, -āre, -āvī, -ātum (*v.t.*) : to ask for, ask.
rūmor, -ōris (*m.*) : rumour, hearsay.
rursus (*adv.*) : again, back, in turn.

săcrificium, -ī (*n.*) : sacrifice.
saepe (*adv.*) : often.
sagitta, -ae (*f.*) : arrow.
sagulum, -ī (*n.*) : cloak.
salūs, -ūtis (*f.*) : safety, well-being.
sanciō, -īre, -nxī, -nctum (*v.t.*) : to bind, ratify; **sanctus, -a, -um :** sacred.
sānus, -a, -um : reasonable; **pro sano facere :** to behave reasonably, like a reasonable being.
sapiō, -ere, -īvī (*v.i.*) : to have sense, understand.
satis (*adv.*) : enough, quite, very; (*subst.* with *gen.*) enough of.
satisfaciō, -ere, -fēcī, -factum (*v.i.*) : to make reparation, give satisfaction; do one's duty to (ch. XXVII).
saucius, -a, -um (*adj.*) : wounded.
scālae, -arum (*f.*) : ladder.
scapha, -ae (*f.*) : skiff, boat.
scelerātus, -a, -um (*adj.*) : vicious, wicked.
scindō, -ere, scidī, scissum (*v.t.*) : to cut, demolish, tear down.
sciō, -īre, -īvī, -ītum (*v.t.*) : to know.
scrībō, -ere, scripsī, scriptum (*v.t.*) : to write.
scūtum, -ī (*n.*) : shield.
sē or **sēsē :** himself, themselves, etc.; **inter se :** mutually.
secundum (*prep.* with *acc.*) : along, by.
secundus, -a, -um : second, favourable, successful.
sed (*conj.*) : but.
sēdēs, -is (*f.*) : seat, settlement, dwelling-place.
semel (*adv.*) : once.
sēmita, -ae (*f.*) : track.
semper (*adv.*) : always.
senātus, -ūs (*m.*) : senate, council.
sententia, -iae (*f.*) : opinion.
sentiō, -īre, sensī, sensum (*v.t.*) : to perceive, realise, think.

septem: seven.
septentriō, -ōnis (*m.*)**:** the Great Bear (*lit.* the seven plough-oxen)**:** (*pl.*) the north.
septimus, -a, -um: seventh.
septingentī, -ae, -a: 700.
sequor, -ī, secutus sum (*v.t.* and *i.*)**:** to follow.
sermō, -ōnis (*m.*)**:** conversation, speech.
sērō (*adv.*)**:** late, too late.
serō, -ere, sēvī, satum (*v.t.*)**:** to sow.
sētius (*comp. adv.*)**:** otherwise; **nihilo setius:** none the less.
servīlis, -e (*adj.*)**:** belonging to *or* of a slave.
servitūs, -ūtis (*f.*)**:** slavery, subjection.
servō, -āre, -āvī, -ātum (*v.t.*)**:** to keep, maintain, watch.
servus, -ī (*m.*)**:** slave.
sēvocō, -āre, -āvī, -ātum (*v.t.*)**:** to call aside, take aside.
sex: six.
sexāgintā: sixty.
sexcentī: 600.
sī (*conj.*)**:** if.
siccitās, -ātis (*f.*)**:** drought, dry state.
sīcut (*adv.*)**:** just as, as if.
sīdus, -eris (*n.*)**:** star, constellation.
significātiō, -ōnis (*f.*)**:** sign, indication, intimation.
signum, -ī (*n.*)**:** standard (Intro., p. 23).
silva, -ae (*f,*)**:** wood, forest.
silvester, -ris, -re: wooded.
similis, -e: like; **similis atque:** the same as.
simul (*adv.*)**:** at the same time; **simul atque:** as soon as.
simulācrum, -ī (*n.*)**:** image.
simulātiō, -ōnis (*f.*)**:** pretence, deceit.
simultās, -ātis (*f.*)**:** rivalry, jealousy.
sīn (*conj.*)**:** but if.
sine (*prep.* with *abl.*)**:** without.
singillātim (*adv.*)**:** individually.
singulāris, -e: one by one, extraordinary, remarkable.
singulī, -ae, -a: one each, one at a time, single.
sinister, -tra, -trum: left, unfavourable.
sinistrorsus (*adv.*)**:** to the left.
sīve or **seu** (*conj.*)**:** whether . . . or.
socius, -iī (*m.*)**:** ally.
sōl, sōlis (*m.*)**:** sun.
soleō, -ēre, -itus sum (*v.i.*)**:** to be accustomed.
solitūdō, inis (*f.*)**:** desert land, lonely place.
sollicitō, -āre, -āvī, -ātum (*v.t.*)**:** to incite, stir up, win over.
sollicitūdō, -inis (*f.*)**:** anxiety.
sōlum (*adv.*)**:** only, alone.
sōlus, -a, -um: only, alone.
solvō, -ere, solvī, solūtum (*v.t.*)**:** to loosen; (**navem**) **solvere:** to set sail, sail out.
spatium, -ī (*n.*)**:** space, time, interval, distance.
speciēs, -ēī (*f.*)**:** appearance, sight, show.
spectō, -āre, -āvī, -ātum (*v.t.*)**:** to look at, look to; **ad meridiem spectat:** faces south.
speculātor, -oris (*m.*)**:** scout.
spērō, -āre, -āvī, -ātum (*v.t.*)**:** to hope for, hope.
spēs, spēī (*f.*)**:** hope.
spoliō, -āre, -āvī, -ātum (*v.t.*)**:** rob of, despoil.
sponte (*abl. fem.*)**:** *with pron. adj.* **mēā, tuā, suā:** of one's own accord, spontaneously.
statim (*adv.*)**:** immediately, at once.

statiō, -ōnis (*f.*) **:** post, station, outpost; **in statione:** on outpost.
statuō, -ere, -uī, -ūtum (*v.t.*) **:** to determine, decide, arrange.
statūra, -ae (*f.*) **:** stature.
status, -ūs (*m.*) **:** situation, condition.
stīpendium, -i (*n.*) **:** tax, tribute, military service.
stō, stāre, stetī, statum (*v.i.*) **:** to stand.
strāmentum, -ī (*n.*) **:** straw, thatch.
strepitus, -ūs (*m.*) **:** clatter, din.
studeō, -ēre, -uī (*v.i.*) **:** to be eager for, apply oneself to.
studiōsē (*adv.*) **:** eagerly, with much pains.
studium, -ī (*n.*) **:** energy, devotion, eagerness.
sub (*prep.* (i) with *abl.*) **:** under; (ii) (with *acc.*) under, up to; **sub brumam:** towards midwinter.
subdūcō, -ere, -duxī, -ductum (*v.t.*) **:** to draw up, beach.
subductiō, -ōnis (*f.*) **:** hauling ashore, beaching.
subiciō, -ere, -iēcī, -iectum (*v.t.*) **:** to place under, expose; **subiectus:** lying near.
subito (*adv.*) **:** hastily, on a sudden.
sublātus, -a, -um: see **tollō.**
subministrō, -āre, -āvī, -ātum (*v.t.*) **:** to supply, furnish.
submittō, -ere, -mīsī, -missum (*v.t.*) **:** to send up, send to help.
subsequor, -ī, -secūtus sum (*v.t.* and *i.*) **:** to follow, to follow on.
subsidium, -ī (*n.*) **:** reserve, relief, help, means of meeting an emergency.
subsistō, -ere, -stitī (*v.i.*) **:** to halt, hold fast.
subsum, -esse (*v.i.*) **:** to be near.
subveniō, -īre, -vēnī, -ventum (*v.i.* with *dat.*) **:** to help, relieve.
succēdō, -ere, -cessī, -cessum (*v.i.*) **:** to come up, succeed, take the place of.
succendō, -ere, -dī, -sum (*v.t.*) **:** to set on fire.
succīdō, -ere, -cīdī, -cīsum (*v.t.*) **:** to cut down.
succurrō, -ere, -currī, -cursum (*v.i.*) **:** to run to the help of (with *dat.*).
sudis, -is (*f.*) **:** stake.
suffrāgium, -ī (*n.*) **:** vote.
sum, esse, fuī: to be.
summa, -ae (*f.*) **:** sum, main part; **summa imperi:** supreme command; **summa belli:** direction of the war.
summus, -a, -um: highest, topmost; **summis copiis contendere** (ch. XVII) **:** to fight with their forces at full strength.
sumptuōsus, -a, -um (*adj.*) **:** costly.
superior, -ius (*comp. adj.*) **:** upper, former, previous.
superō, -āre, -āvī, -ātum (*v.t.*) **:** to subdue, conquer.
supersum, -esse, -fuī (*v.i.*) **:** to remain over, survive.
superus, -a, -um (*comp.*) **: superior, -ius:** (*superl.*) **: supremus** and **summus:** high, upper.
supplicium, -ī (*n.*) **:** punishment.
suprā (*adv.*, and *prep.* with *acc.*) **:** above.
suspiciō, -ōnis (*f.*) **:** suspicion, imputation.

suspicor, -ārī, -ātus sum (*v.t.*) : to suspect.
sustentō, -āre, -āvī, -ātum (*v.t.*) : to endure, support.
sustineō, -ēre, -tinuī, -tentum (*v.t.*) : to withstand, hold out against.
suus, -a, -um : his own, their own, etc.

tālea, -ae (*f.*) : bar, ingot.
tālis, -e (*adj.*) : such.
tam (*adv.*) : so, so much.
tamen (*adv.*) : nevertheless, however, yet.
tametsi (*conj.*) : although.
tandem (*adv.*) : at length.
tangō, -ere, tetigī, tactum (*v.t.*) : to touch, border on.
tantulus, -a, -um : so little, so trifling.
tantum (*adv.*) : so much, only.
tantus, -a, -um : so great; (*subst.*) **tantum** : so much.
tardē,-ius,-issimē (*adv.*) : slowly.
tegimentum, -ī (*n.*) : covering.
tegō, -ere, texī, tectum (*v.t.*) : to roof, cover, hide.
tēlum, -ī (*n.*) : missile.
temerārius, -a, -um (*adj.*) : rash, headstrong.
temere (*adv.*) : rashly, lightly, without good reason.
temeritās, -ātis (*f.*) : rashness, recklessness.
temperātus, -a, -um : mild, of equable climate.
tempestās, -ātis (*f.*) : storm, gale, weather.
temptō, -āre, -āvī, -ātum (*v.t.*) : to try, tempt.
tempus, -oris (*n.*) : time; **ad tempus** : in the nick of time.
teneō, -ēre, -uī, tentum (*v.t.*) : to hold; **cursum tenere** : to keep one's course.
tenuis, -e (*adj.*) : weak, thin, worthless.
tergum, -ī (*n.*) : back, rear.
terra, -ae (*f.*) : earth, land, country.
terreō, -ēre, -uī, -itum (*v.t.*) : to frighten.
territō, -āre, -āvī, -ātum (*v.t.*) : to frighten, intimidate.
terror, -ōris (*m.*) : fright, alarm.
tertius, -a, -um : third.
tertius decimus : thirteenth.
testimōnium, -ī (*n.*) : proof, evidence, report of a general (ch. LII).
testūdō, -inis (*f.*) : tortoise, a mobile shelter for troops; see p. 83.
timeō, -ēre -uī (*v.t.* and *i.*) : to fear, be alarmed.
timidē (*adv.*) : nervously, faintheartedly.
timor, -ōris (*m.*) : fear, panic.
tolerō, -āre, -āvī, -ātum (*v.t.*) : to endure, sustain.
tollō, -ere, sustulī, sublātum (*v.t.*) : to lift, raise; **ancoras tollere** : to weigh anchor.
tormentum, -ī (*n.*) : a military engine for throwing missiles, artillery.
torreō, -ēre, -uī, tostum (*v.t.*) : to scorch, burn.
tot : so many.
tōtus, -a, -um : whole, entire.
trādō, -ere, -didī, -ditum (*v.t.*) : to give up, deliver, pass on.
trādūcō, -ere, -duxī, -ductum (*v.t.*) : to cross, convey across, bring over.
trāgula, -ae (*f.*) : javelin.
trāiciō, -ere, -iēcī, -iectum (*v.t.*) : to pierce.
trāiectus, -ūs (*m.*) : crossing, passage.
tranquillitās, -ātis (*f.*) : calm.

trans (*prep.* with *acc.*) **:** across, beyond.
transeō, -īre, -iī, -itum (*v.i.*) **:** to go over, cross.
transferō, -ferre, -tulī, -lātum (*v.t.*) **:** to transfer.
transfīgō, -ere, -fixī, -fixum (*v.t.*) **:** to pierce through, transfix.
transitus, -ūs (*m.*) **:** crossing, passage.
transmarīnus, -a, -um (*adj.*) **:** oversea, imported.
transmissus, -ūs (*m.*) **:** passage.
transportō, -āre, -āvī, -ātum (*v.t.*) **:** to carry over.
trecentī, -ae, -a : 300.
trepidō, -āre, -āvī, -ātum (*v.i.*) **:** to fuss, bustle about anxiously.
trēs, tria : three.
tribunus, -ī (*m.*) **:** tribune (see Intro., p. 24).
tribuō, -ere, tribuī, tribūtum (*v.t.*) **:** to assign, bestow; **tantum dignitatis tribuere** (ch. VII) **:** to attach so much importance to.
tribūtum, -ī (*n.*) **:** tax.
trīgintā : thirty.
trīnī, -ae, -a : three each, three.
tripertīto (*adv.*) **:** in three divisions.
triquetrus, -a, -um : triangular.
tueor, -ērī, tuitus sum (*v.t.*) **:** to defend, protect.
tum (*adv.*) **:** then; **cum . . . tum :** not only . . . but also . . .
tumultus, -us (*m.*) **:** confusion, commotion, rising.
tumulus, -ī (*m.*) **:** hill, mound.
turma, -ae (*f.*) **:** troop, squadron.
turpis, -e (*adj.*) **:** disgraceful, shameful.
turris, -is (*f.*) **:** tower.
tūtus, -a, -um (*adj.*) **:** safe.

ubī (*conj.*) **:** when, where; **ubi primum :** as soon as.
ulciscor, -ī, ultus sum (*v.t.*) **:** take vengeance on, punish.
ullus, -a, -um : any.
ulterior, -ius (*comp. adj.*) **:** outer, farther; (*superl.*) **ultimus :** last, farthest.
ultrō (*adv.*) **:** voluntarily, of one's own accord, actually, going beyond what one might expect, into the bargain.
ululātus, -us (*m.*) **:** yell.
ūnā (*adv.*) **:** together.
unde (*adv.*) **:** whence, from which.
undecimus, -a, -um : eleventh.
undique (*adv.*) **:** from all parts, on every side.
ūniversus, -a, -um : all together, massed.
unquam (*adv.*) **:** ever, at any time.
ūnus, -a, -um : one, alone.
usque (*adv.*) **:** even, quite, as far as.
ūsus, -ūs (*m.*) **:** experience, practice, use; **usui esse :** to be serviceable, useful; **ex usu esse :** to be advantageous.
ut or **utī** (*adv.* and *conj.*) **:** how, as, as though, since, when, in order that, so that.
uter, utra, utrum : which of two.
uterque, utraque, utrumque : both.
ūtor, -ī, ūsus sum (*v.i.* with *abl.*) **:** use, show, enjoy, benefit by.
uxor, -ōris (*f.*) **:** wife.

vadum, -ī (*n.*) **:** foal, shoal.
vāgīna, -ae (*f.*) **:** scabbard. sheath.
vagor, -ārī, -ātus sum (*v.i.*) **:** to wander.

valeō, -ēre, -uī (*v.i.*) : to be strong, have influence.
valetūdō, -inis (*f.*) : health, infirmity.
vallis, -is (*f.*) : valley.
vallum, -ī (*n.*) : palisade, rampart (see p. oo).
varietās, -ātis (*f.*) : diversity, variety.
vastō, -āre, -āvī, -ātum (*v.t.*) : to lay waste.
vectīgal, -ālis (*n.*) : tax, tribute.
vectōrius, -a, -um : for transport.
vel (*conj.* and *adv.*) : or, even; **vel . . . vel . . .** : either . . . or . . .
vēlōcitās, -ātis (*f.*) : speed.
vēlōciter, -ōcius, -ōcissimē (*adv.*) : swiftly.
veniō, -īre, vēnī, ventum (*v.i.*) : to come.
ventitō, -āre, -āvī, -ātum (*v.i.*) : to come and go.
ventus, -ī (*m.*) : wind.
verbum, -ī (*n.*) : word.
vereor, -ērī, -itus sum (*v.t.*) : to fear, fear for.
vergō, -ere (*v.i.*) : to lean, tie, slope; **vergit ad Hispaniam** (ch. XIII) : faces Spain.
vērō (*adv.*) : in truth, but, however.
versō, -āre, -āvī, -ātum (*v.t.*) : to turn often, move about, play with; (*pass.*) move about, be active, mix (with people).
vertō, -ere, vertī, versum (*v.t.*) : to turn.
vērus, -a, -um : true.
verūtum, -ī (*n.*) : dart, javelin.
vesper, -eris and **-erī** (*m.*) : evening.
vestīgium, -ī (*n.*) : footprint, track.
vestiō, -īre, -īvī, -ītum (*v.t.*) : to clothe.
vetō, -āre, -uī, -itum (*v.t.*) : to forbid.
vetus, -eris (*adj.*) : old, veteran.
via, -ae (*f.*(: road, route, way.
vīciēs (*adv.*) : twenty times.
victor, -ōris (*m.*) : conqueror.
victōria, -ae (*f.*) : victory.
victus, -ūs (*m.*) : living, victuals.
videō, -ēre, vīdī, vīsum (*v.t.*) : to see; (*pass.*) to be seen, seem, appear.
vigilia, -ae (*f.*) : watch.
vīgintī : twenty.
vīmen, -inis (*n.*) : twig, osier, wicker-work.
vincō, -ere, vīcī, victum (*v.t.*) : to conquer.
vinculum, -ī (*n.*) : chain; (*pl.*) prison.
violō, -āre, -āvī, -ātum (*v.t.*) : to do violence to, ill-treat.
vir, virī (*m.*) : man, husband.
virgō, -inis (*f.*) : maiden.
virtūs, -ūtis (*f.*) : valour, courage, merit.
vīs, vim, vī, *pl.* **vīres** (*f.*) : violence, strength.
vīta, -ae (*f.*) : life.
vītō, -āre, -āvī, -ātum (*v.t.*) : to avoid.
vītrum, -ī (*n.*) : woad.
vīvō, -ere, vīxī, victum (*v.i.*) : to live; (with *abl.*) to live on.
vix (*adv.*) : barely, scarcely.
vocō, -āre, -āvī, -ātum (*v.t.*) : to call, summon.
volō, velle, voluī (*v.t.* and *i.*) : to wish, be willing, mean.
voluntārius, -a, -um (*adj.*) : of one's own free will; (*subst.*) volunteer.
voluntās, -ātis (*f.*) : will, inclination, goodwill.

voluptās, -ātis (*f.*) : pleasure, amusement.
vōs : you.
voveō, -ēre, vōvī, vōtum (*v.t.*) : to vow.
vox, vōcis (*f.*) : voice, word.
vulgo (*adv.*) : generally, often.
vulgus, -ī (*n.*) : the common people, populace.
vulnerō, -āre, -āvī, -ātum (*v.t.*) : to wound.
vulnus, -eris (*n.*) : wound.

Printed in the USA
CPSIA information can be obtained
at www.ICGtesting.com
LVHW011239310723
753902LV00002B/109